The Pursuit of Purpose

Meditations on Life Lessons

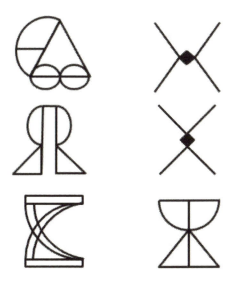

Garrett Kincaid

All the best,
Garrett Kincaid

Copyright © 2019 by Garrett Kincaid

All rights reserved. This book or any portion thereof may not be reproduced or used in any manner whatsoever without the expressed written permission of the publisher except for the use of brief quotations in a book review or scholarly journal.

Place of Publication: Hoboken, NJ

ISBN: 9781689827089
Library of Congress Control Number: 2019915997

Cover art by Gregory Concha

garrettkincaidauthor.com

To my parents and sister, without whom I would not even desire to have these thoughts.

Written in memory of Joel Diffendaffer;
may his light and love endure forever.

CONTENTS

›	WARM-UP	VII
›	LESSONS	XIII
›	CEREMONIAL FIRST PITCH	XXVII
1	MINDSET: Framing Your Perspective	1
2	CONFIDENCE: Fuel for the Mind	28
3	CHARACTER: Your Internal Roadmap	43
4	INTERACTIONS: Incrementing Your Impact	58
5	REALATIONSHIPS: Vehicles for Enjoyment and Fulfillment	78
6	AMBITIONS: The Peaks of Life's Mountain Range	96
›	EXTRA INNINGS	113

WARM-UP

Of anything, my education has played the single greatest part in forming my perspective. Education is a priority for my parents, and they have made great sacrifices to provide my sister and me with one of high quality. The value that I place on education is just one of the many aspects of my character that I attribute to my parents. In large part, this book is an attempt to determine how I need to act in order to emulate my parents and provide similar opportunities for my own children in the future. I have nothing but gratitude for what my parents have taught me; they have provided incredible examples as individuals and as parents. I hope to take what I have learned and apply it to the highest degree possible. The general aim of this book is to develop a personal philosophy—a way of living—that will allow me to be the best person that I can be for myself, for others, and as a parent to my future-children.

As I said, it starts with education. Academia is rife with profound ideas and eloquent explanations that urge me to define priorities, goals, and beliefs of my own. My education has exposed me to countless interpretations of the world, and in synthesizing those interpretations, I have defined the world in two ways: quantitatively and qualitatively. The world is quantified by fields such as physics, biology, chemistry, and mathematics. The same is done qualitatively by way of politics, literature, history, and philosophy. However, knowledge is not limited to the observed world. In fact, a perfect and exhaustive understanding of the physical universe does not begin to approach the boundaries of knowledge, for, within each person, there is a universe of equal depth and complexity. The only exhaustive pursuit of knowledge is one that includes both exploration and introspection. This book is the product of my own introspective journey.

During my freshman year of high school in history class, I learned that Marcus Aurelius, the emperor of Rome during the second century, wrote a collection of essays that is now called *Meditations*. He documented lessons to which he attributed a great amount of personal development. These were lessons that he wanted to pass on to his sons, so he recorded them in a single volume.

Even though I learned about Aurelius during my freshman year, it was not until sophomore year that I began my own list of lessons. The record of these lessons started as a note on my phone, and the first entry was the "Golden Rule." Upon recording that first entry, I recalled Marcus Aurelius from freshman year and titled the note "Lessons: (Meditations)." After inputting the Golden Rule, I recorded my first original lesson and then wrote ninety-nine more during the two-and-a-half-year period that followed.

At one point, about midway through the list of lessons, I decided that I would compile them in the form of a book and address each one. I do not want a record of these lessons because I fear that I will abandon my principles. Rather, I want it to serve as a moral foundation to build upon in the future. At its conception, this book was meant to act solely as a personal point of reference—I had not planned on sharing it. However, after having family and close friends encourage me to publish it, I decided to do so. I am glad that I decided to share my thoughts because it demanded a more refined explanation of my philosophy that had to be clear to others, not just clear to me. The challenge of an audience helped me refine and bolster my perspective, filling logical holes and sharpening my own understanding of it. The added component of an audience also gave the book more of a purpose; instead of just a record of my introspection for my own uses, the book can now be seen as a testimonial to the power and potential benefits of introspection.

Although I do strongly believe in my own philosophy and perspective, I do not wish to command the actions of anyone but myself. In the following pages, I am not promoting my perspective or demanding one interpretation of it; I am merely presenting my view in the hopes that it encourages introspective thought and the conscious consideration of certain ideas. My hope is that you do not emulate or adopt these ideas outright but consider them in the context of your own perspective. Know that, when I use "you" in the book, I am really addressing my future-self.

Directly following this preface is my list of lessons—the foundation of my introspective journey. The lessons are sequentially numbered and appear in the order that I originally conceived them. In the body of the work, each lesson is placed into one of six chapters: "Mindset," "Confidence," "Character," "Interactions," "Relationships," and "Ambitions." I view each lesson as a distinct, gift-wrapped package. The sight of the package summons an idea, but the contents of it allow you to apply that idea. Throughout the book, explanations of each lesson work to reveal the contents of every package.

In relaying these explanations, my primary consideration is the combination of clarity and concision. I hope to achieve clarity by not clouding the page with text that does not serve the purpose of explanation; I want each word to serve the lesson at hand. Clarity, in this sense, is not characterized by concrete imagery or a spoon-fed meaning. It is more like the clarity found in poetry—the clarity of concepts. Most poetry is proficient at being clear without restricting the reader to a rigid, inelastic meaning. I want the lessons and the relationships between them to be interpretable, like poems. Where an idea may be concrete, I want the potential applications of that idea to be wide-ranging. I hope that I am concise, for concision, in conjunction with clarity, allows the reader to efficiently extrapolate meaning.

I have my own aspirations for how I want this book to benefit me, but I also have certain hopes regarding its impact on you, the reader. Namely, I hope that this book promotes discussion. The discussion of challenging ideas is uniquely enriching; there is an unmatched satisfaction and observable growth that comes from concluding a definition for a complex idea or from arriving at a solution to a puzzling problem. The best interactions are challenging and enriching. I measure the success of a day largely by the quality of my interactions, for interacting is how you learn and grow. Hopefully this book sparks enriching conversations among its readers, spurring realizations that incite further introspection.

In my experience with introspection, I have found that conclusions cannot be forced; they must form over time. Introspection is organic and fluid, and what may seem out of place in a moment will eventually take its place in the greater form of self-understanding. In an attempt to give further context to my own introspection, the lessons in the book are assigned a chronological number and are only referenced in conjunction with it. This structural choice serves two purposes: (1) it allows for quick reference between a lesson in the list and its explanation in the book, and (2) it highlights the long-term, fluid nature of introspection when two neighboring lessons' numbers indicate that they were written months or years apart. This structure should provide both a macro and micro view of my introspection.

I have taken the time and spent the effort to identify and articulate my personal philosophy, and it has been the most enriching endeavor imaginable. I now have a clearer idea of who I am and of who I want to become. My hope is that this book can provide some degree of inspiration, motivation, or thoughts for consideration that aid you in your own pursuits.

LESSONS:

1. Always allow for the benefit of the doubt. *pg 58*

2. Be open to changing your opinion, or else your opinion becomes biased or ill-informed. *pg 7*

3. Gather as much information as possible before passing judgment in any situation. *pg 60*

4. Keep objects that remind you of the past and collections that continue into the future. *pg 82*

5. Continually be aware of your interests, desires, and goals. *pg 96*

6. Find a purpose for what you do that is bigger than yourself by honoring the sacrifices that others have made for you and taking advantage of every opportunity they provide. *pg 110*

7. Never be afraid to engage with people. You never know what a new relationship or a single interaction could bring. *pg 80*

8. Ask often and wonder freely. Everyone shares in uncertainty, and others likely have the same questions that you do. A common concern could lead to an interaction, a relationship, or a solution. *pg 83*

9. Respect the game; no excuses. *pg 43*

10. Being stressed is a choice that is determined by your outlook, so find a positive outlook that allows you to accomplish your work while not feeling stressed or weighed down by it. *pg 17*

11. Learn from every failure to ensure success in the future. *pg 55*

12. The truth trumps all; honesty is always beneficial, whether it be in the short run or in the long run. *pg 54*

13. The key to confidence is the ability to justify your actions and opinions with your own beliefs, experiences, and logic; it comes from knowing yourself and never wavering from your principles. *pg 30*

14. Strive for eternal optimism. *pg 2*

15. Competition provides some of the most valuable experiences, as well as long-lasting life lessons. *pg 98*

16. Do not exude false confidence regarding a matter of which you lack knowledge. Doing so is a form of dishonesty, for people will believe what you say if it is said with confidence. *pg 32*

17. Accelerate to escape someone's blind spot. Do not slow down and fall back into their rear-view mirror. Seize opportunities, take control, and make yourself known. Do not allow others to determine your position. *pg 62*

18. Having confidence in your abilities is the first step toward success, and the truest form of confidence results from preparation and practice. *pg 39*

19. The pursuit of scientific knowledge is the pursuit of human progress. *pg 98*

20. Teach how to think, not what to think. *pg 84*

21. Outward expressions of passion and dedication result in respect and admiration from others. *pg 62*

22. Courage is uncommon, and witnessing courage increases motivation and self-confidence. *pg 36*

23. Any negative reaction to your personal expression or achievement is just others' way of justifying why they did not do it themselves. *pg 10*

24. Lead people; never demean people. *pg 63*

25. Remind friends of their inner potential and aptitude, ensuring that they acknowledge their own greatness. *pg 92*

26. The more constants there are, the more comfortable and stress-free life will be. Try to limit uncertainty in your daily actions by establishing routines and increasing your overall efficiency. *pg 16*

27. Acknowledge a need for change, progress, reform etc., but be conscious and reminded of the positive aspects of each situation. *pg 20*

28. Do not sacrifice your beliefs or priorities in order to accomplish a short-term goal or to be more compatible with another person. Use your unique personality and unwavering character to be successful in your own pursuits. *pg 53*

29. Philosophers do not sit on the beach, peering from the shore. They climb a mountain to gaze upon all that leads to the shore and the entire sea beyond. *pg 19*

30. Your name will only be recorded in history if you act to impact the future. *pg 23*

31. Possibly the greatest pursuit in life is that of knowledge and the application of discovered truths. *pg 99*

32. Squeeze Theorem applied to life: No individual is more important than you, and you are no less important than any other individual. If you are not greater nor lesser, then you are equal. *pg 10*

33. Privilege should not be met with guilt but rather with inherent ambition and a sense of responsibility to better the world. *pg 11*

34. Places are the stuff of the most vivid memories. Experience places in an intimate way, and use those places to form more intimate relationships with the people that you share them with. *pg 81*

35. Human progress is like wading through water with variable depth. The water accumulates at a constant rate, but the rate at which it drains varies. When the drain is clogged by stagnation, monotony, or conflict, the water level rises, making it harder to move forward. Conversely, when there is discovery, innovation, or revolution, the drain is cleared, and the water level lowers to a much more manageable depth. Prioritize progress so that humanity may wade forth with ease. *pg 100*

36. Events and actions in the past are what determine the present, but you, in the now, determine the future. *pg 14*

37. At any instant, you only have control of what happens in a moment of time and in a sliver of space, but the sum of those instants yields your experience and impact. *pg 22*

38. Never feel entitled to respect; it must be earned and achieved on an individual basis. *pg 93*

39. Know that you are worthy of being heard, of being wherever you are or aspire to be, and of belonging wherever you may be. Own it, and no one will question your place. *pg 14*

40. Prioritize quality over quantity. Realize that in some instances, though, the highest level of quality is achieved by the most efficient route to quantity. *pg 25*

41. Maximize efficiency. Define what efficiency is to you, and know that it is dependent on both quality and quantity. Coordinate your actions and processes accordingly. *pg 24*

42. Travel so that unfamiliar places and situations become more comfortable and common. *pg 102*

43. Be devout in your own greatness. *pg 28*

44. Address it. *pg 59*

45. Heed the voices of history; the brevity of human existence is most evident in the relevance of elder commentaries. *pg 87*

46. Never become numb to change, yet accept it as part of nature. *pg 20*

47. The best time in life is now. *pg 26*

48. Achieve autonomous motivation for unified progress. *pg 46*

49. Express gratitude, and do not expect it. *pg 93*

50. Refrain from attribution and accept responsibility. *pg 53*

51. Expand your own realms of comfort and knowledge so that you may know more and do more in the future and in the present. *pg 101*

52. Be sound and thorough in your thoughts so that the words and actions to follow are congruent. *pg 48*

53. You must truly know yourself in order to dutifully interact with others. *pg 68*

54. People are interested in what you have to say and if they are not, they will be once you say it. *pg 40*

55. Do not wish ill on others, for that action distracts you from your own pursuits of happiness, knowledge, and self-improvement. *pg 90*

56. Before taking action in any situation, ensure that your motivations are in accordance with your own nature. *pg 47*

57. Fears of death preserve life, but fears of living inhibit it. *pg 34*

58. Limit auxiliary interactions by exchanging pleasantries, making personal inquiries, and forming intimate connections. *pg 64*

59. Guilt is the most invasive and pervasive sentiment. It tethers the mind to the past through the recollection of regretful actions. To be unrestrained by guilt, address your regrets and make penance. *pg 72*

60. Change is the universal nature; it is an inescapable fact. By this, stagnation is impossible. If you are not experiencing positive progress, then you are falling behind. *pg 9*

61. You should be reliable and involved in each engagement to the point where your absence is noticed and your presence is felt. *pg 51*

62. Objects at rest tend to stay at rest unless acted upon by an external force, and conversation is such an object. Exert a force to accelerate that object and put conversation in motion, for objects in motion tend to stay in motion. *pg 66*

63. Avoid the creation and the indulgence of perverse incentives; the former happens by chance or results from a lack of analysis or understanding, and the latter benefits neither individuals nor the common good. *pg 5*

64. Your principles and character grow strong as a tree does resisting the force of the wind. Remain resolute in spite of adversity. *pg 52*

65. You could rely on changing yourself in the future, or you could change right now. The only way to become who you are supposed to be in the future is to be who you want to be in the present. *pg 97*

66. The macro is made in the micro; there is a process in everything, and a desirable outcome cannot be reached without complete effort throughout the process. *pg 13*

67. What hinders you? Ask this question of yourself when you are discouraged, and be honest. The most likely case is that any hindrance you identify is just an excuse. *pg 56*

68. Your trajectory can be altered by external forces, but the severity of their impact is under your control. If you limit the weight of negative forces and limit the time that you dwell on them, their effect will be dampened. This practice is entirely necessary if you are to retain command over your path in life. *pg 55*

69. Assuming benevolent intentions, the only regrettable actions are those done in the absence of complete effort or as a result of oversight. *pg 50*

70. It is not enough to know that you respect someone; they must know it too. *pg 91*

71. Know yourself well so that you are able to detect incongruences in your actions, as to not damage your relationships with others. *pg 78*

72. Ignorance is bliss, but knowledge is freedom. Prefer the latter. *pg 6*

73. The most suspicious, accusatory individuals are those who have either been a victim or a culprit. *pg 61*

74. Immoral actions are more often caused by the practice of irrational justification than by flawed morality. *pg 48*

75. In spite of resistance, redirect current to illuminate a bulb that shines brighter than the rest. *pg 42*

76. If you did not get better at something, then you wasted a day. *pg 102*

77. You should only make connections with dynamic entities because change is inevitable. It is detrimental to your personal progress to associate with static entities, for anything averse to change is contrary to nature. *pg 88*

78. Busyness is healthy and constructive; it helps develop the important skill of time management. *pg 104*

79. Do not work to become famous. Become famous for your work. *pg 22*

80. Death is but an instant in the eternal breath of your life and legacy. *pg 25*

81. The time you have to impact the world is finite, but the ramifications of your actions are infinite. *pg 76*

82. Encourage the successes of others; resenting their success will tempt the creation of excuses or a lack of self-confidence. *pg 41*

83. Celebrate progress instead of cursing incompletion. *pg 4*

84. Widen the breadth of your experience so that you may hone the accuracy of your empathy. *pg 79*

85. Saturate your experiences with your attention so that you forge more vivid memories. *pg 18*

86. Do not change yourself, find yourself. *pg 41*

87. Failing due to fear is destructive, but trying and failing is constructive. *pg 69*

88. There is duality in everything. Understand extremes so that you can achieve balance. *pg 103*

89. Perpetuate and encourage the thoughts and actions that you wish to see in the world. *pg 67*

90. The fuel for your actions should come from within, not from recognition or external validation. *pg 31*

91. Never expect more of others than you do of yourself. *pg 108*

92. No one thing should constantly consume your thoughts. Engage in all of your interests, and be well-rounded so that you avoid resenting your own priorities. *pg 106*

93. Live in a time that is balanced between your past and future. Do not long for the past but be willing to relive it. Do not rush to the future but be sure to enjoy it when it comes. *pg 24*

94. Long to be held accountable. *pg 31*

95. Good-natured people will respect you for having independent views rather than disrespect you because your views differ. *pg 88*

96. In each indulgence, congruence should take precedence over quantity. *pg 105*

97. Pain should act as a catalyst. If you allow pain to become injury, it, instead, hinders progress. *pg 21*

98. The human experience is defined by ups and downs, and *a* human's experience is defined by their response to those extremes. *pg 15*

99. Employ logos and pathos to solidify your ethos, or credibility. Do not assume that your credibility is recognized or accepted; prove it by

logically explaining your methods and clearly illustrating your passions. *pg 74*

100. Be open with others; vulnerability is not synonymous with weakness. *pg 94*

CEREMONIAL FIRST PITCH

"Treat others the way you would like to be treated."

This lesson is all-encompassing, versatile, and a sound foundation on which to build a personal philosophy. Yes, the Golden Rule is undeniably cliché, but the defining characteristic of clichés is repetition. A phrase is only frequently repeated if people agree with its message, and few refute the good-natured notion of the clichéd Golden Rule. However, many do not spend enough time with this rule to move past its concision and perceived simplicity. The path to adhering to the Golden Rule involves both introspection and empathy; you must know how you want to be treated as well as how others want to be treated.

The first step—self-reflection—is difficult because it requires unique, conscious, and continuous effort. It can be daunting to attempt to define your personal beliefs and desires. A large part of this effort of discovery lies in the process of reflecting on your past experiences. Identify the experiences that were the most influential in shaping your personality and perspective. What characteristics do you value in others? What are the most impactful relationships in your life? What sort of interactions do you find to be the most enriching? By asking yourself these questions, you will start to characterize desirable experiences. A desirable experience could be as simple as finding a new food or as complex as forming a deep connection with another person. Define what makes an experience desirable to you. Is it one that yields new knowledge? Is it one that makes you laugh? Work to create impactful, enriching experiences for yourself. This may seem intuitive; for acting on your own desires is often done without much conscious effort. However, ensure that your definition of a desirable experience is one that does not deviate from your nature or from your morals. You will act to create desirable experiences, so be sure that you truly understand what you desire and what you hope to achieve.

The next step in implementing the Golden Rule is rooted in empathy. In addition to introspection, the Golden Rule demands that you are conscious of others and aware of how your actions affect the world around you. Yes, treat others as you would want them to treat you; that is a good start. In order to go beyond that, though, you must exert the necessary effort to learn how *others* want to be treated. Enter empathy.

It is likely that others would prefer to be treated differently than you would like to be. This disparity of preferences and perspectives is evident in the fact that people characterize desirable experiences differently. Others' priorities and preferences should not be overlooked when you are deciding how to interact with them. The Golden Rule could be rewritten to highlight this idea: "Treat others the way you would like to be treated *if you were them.*" If you are to act dutifully and in accordance with the Golden Rule, it is essential to combine your self-understanding with an understanding of others. Empathy should stem from the shared human truth that each individual is unique. Strengthen your empathy by identifying others' ideas, priorities, preferences, interests and relating them to your own. To relate to others, you must be conscious and sure of your own nature while being attuned to the information that others share about themselves.

Focus on developing deep, interpersonal connections because everyone longs for such relationships; they are incredibly enriching. In relationships of both brevity and longevity, realize others' uniqueness, and treat them as you would want to be treated if you were them.

Employ the Golden Rule as an omnipresent, foundational guideline for your own processes of self-discovery and personal growth. Direct your personal growth toward the primary aspects of your being: mindset, confidence, character, interactions, relationships, and ambitions. Your mindset is defined by the experiences you wish to create, relationships are forged by shared interactions, and confidence is tempered by character. Then, character poises you to achieve your ambitions. These factors are all within your control. Define who you are and become who you want to be.

LET'S PLAY BALL

MINDSET:
FRAMING YOUR PERSPECTIVE

14. Strive for eternal optimism.

External influences have the potential to affect your disposition, and they will constantly bombard you in an attempt to do so. However, in spite of those potential influences, you must choose to retain control of your outlook. Realize the power that you have over your emotions and determine your own perspective. This is not to say that your emotions should be diluted or ignored for the sake of positivity. Diluting your emotions will dilute your passions, and to lack passion is to lack a route to purpose. Achieve a positive outlook by engaging in your passions and by being hopeful that they will lead you to purpose.

Hope breeds optimism. Without hope—without trust in the future—your outlook in the present will be negative and pessimistic.

Optimism demands action; you must consciously address your thoughts and feelings in a way that results in a positive, hopeful outlook. You cannot control your initial emotional responses, but you can control how you react to them. Those controlled reactions are what shape your perception. Work to achieve a desirable outlook. What is the alternative? Your mental state is within your control, so will you allow yourself to have a pessimistic view? Your mental state will only become uncontrollable if you believe that it is out of your control.

In the active pursuit of optimism, you should not prioritize it over realism or knowledge. Do not achieve positivity and hope by choosing to ignore the threatening and disheartening parts of the world. Acknowledge the entirety of reality, but temper your disposition by controlling your reactions to it. Ignorance and naiveté are hinderances; they detract from reasoning and exploration. You must preserve and prioritize your ability to reason as well as your desire to explore, so do not entertain ignorance. Control the thoughts and reactions that your mind indulges in. Make them positive!

There is a clear distinction between a fleeting feeling of optimism and achieving eternal optimism. Merely fabricating optimism, in the moment, suggests that you are ignoring parts of reality. Being eternally optimistic requires conscious and constant effort; it is a practice that is developed by finding the positive aspects of every experience and learning to retain hope in spite of adversity. An eternally optimistic outlook is beneficial because it fuels your imagination with hope and fortifies your confidence with positivity.

Optimism is not something that you can simply claim to have or that you can inadvertently acquire. Constantly make an effort to find silver linings, recognize best-case scenarios, and retain hope. Optimism should be a fundamental part of and guiding principle for your mindset.

83. Celebrate progress instead of cursing incompletion. If your end goal is to be renowned for your accomplishments, you may become hyper-focused on the horizon and lose sight of what is at hand. Establish a hierarchy of goals so that your focus is concentrated in the moment while ensuring that your actions are directed toward your long-term aspirations. By only ever considering the finish line, you will inevitably be dissatisfied with your progress. While disappointment can serve as motivation, continuous dissatisfaction negatively affects your confidence and your ability to progress. You will feel the same degree of incompletion at the half mile marker of a one mile run as you do 13.1 miles through a marathon. However, one is significantly more difficult to complete than the other. Do not let what you have yet to achieve overshadow that which you have already accomplished.

Satisfaction is relative to expectation. If you expect to succeed immediately, then you will be perpetually dissatisfied, and that will impact your motivation to progress. However, you should not set your expectations too low in an effort to avoid dissatisfaction altogether. Momentary dissatisfaction can drive you forward. Set high expectations that compel you to put forth effort and focus. Gradually progress toward your goals; do not look to achieve them outright.

While working through your hierarchy of goals, acknowledge the progress that you have already made. You will be more productive and happier as a result.

63. Avoid the creation and the indulgence of perverse incentives; the former happens by chance or results from a lack of analysis or understanding, and the latter benefits neither individuals nor the common good. For an incentive to be perverse, it must provoke an action that opposes an objectively desirable outcome. A perfect example of such an incentive would be the NBA draft lottery. The best chance to obtain the first pick in the draft is awarded to the team with the worst record for that season. In any given season, for any team, a high win percentage and a good record is a desirable outcome, but it is one that is not incentivized by the process of determining the draft order. Obviously, the draft lottery is organized such that struggling teams have a better chance to have more success in the future. The direct effect of this system is that, toward the end of the season, struggling teams are motivated to lose games. When teams know that they have no shot at the playoffs, their primary focus becomes restructuring their team for the next season, and therefore, they prioritize their position in the draft order above winning games. That is an indication of a perverse incentive because winning is an objectively desirable outcome.

Given the binary option of a win or a loss, a win is objectively preferable, but incentives can pervert priorities and skew outcomes. Perverse incentives arise not just in the world of sports, but in politics, business, and social interactions. Perverse incentives should be avoided or remedied to ensure sound motivations for every action.

72. Ignorance is bliss, but knowledge is freedom. Prefer the latter. While it may be enticing or seemingly sensible to be ignorant, you must choose to know and actively seek the truth. To ignore the people around you is to be selfish and apathetic. To ignore the ramifications of your actions is to be parasitic. To ignore the nature of the world is to be voluntarily imprisoned. The pursuit of knowledge gives you direction, experience, and insight. Do not forsake those things merely to feel comfortable in the world.

It is common and acceptable to view yourself as the protagonist of your life's narrative. Do not, however, allow yourself to be a protagonist that is defined only by being in opposition to an antagonist. Since the common, archetypal narrative is to have a protagonist vs. an antagonist, people are inclined to highlight and inflate the flaws or wrongdoings of those who have wronged them. Many people look for an enemy to combat in their narrative. This search for opposition feeds the idea that everything is defined by its opposite. If you are not strongly in opposition to one thing, then what are you for? Instead, why not support an entirely unique viewpoint that is partially in opposition and partially in favor of another's view? Yin does not oppose yang; rather, yin and yang exist harmoniously in one being. You should be in complete support of your own beliefs, but they should not be characterized by opposing and negating some other belief. Conflicting ideas should balance and complement each other, synthesizing into your unique view of the world.

To vehemently and outrightly oppose the entirety of someone's view is to be closed-minded and ignorant of the common ground that you share with others. You should not view others' perspectives as a protagonist views an antagonist. Opposing views are more akin to competitors or teachers than they are to enemies; they are necessary, and you can learn from them. Individuality cannot exist without the process of learning and growth. That process is stunted by closed-mindedness. If the extremes of opinion are defined by voluntary ignorance of all opposing views, then no one on those extremes can be considered a true individual. Failing to be open-minded encourages group-thought and a subscription to a group mentality; that is the clearest diversion from individuality. Employ open-mindedness and due consideration to remain an independent thinker.

If you consider yourself to be an independent individual and the protagonist of your own narrative, then your enemy—the antagonist—should be ignorance. The extremes of thought are only cultivated by those that dismiss the opposition and remain ignorant to the merits of contradictory arguments. Choose to know many perspectives, do not reject any counterarguments without due consideration, and synthesize your own, independent view.

2. Be open to changing your opinion, or else your opinion becomes biased or ill-informed. It is difficult to remain optimistic when what you know to be true is disproven. An unexpected change

in your understanding of the world can cause you to be unsure of where to look to or how to react. Do not reject that new knowledge; that is not the answer. Be proud of your beliefs, but do not be averse to change merely because of that pride. If you reject change, your pride will morph into stubbornness and ignorance. Recognize that change is the natural order of all things. If you are impervious to adjusting your own convictions, you will not bend with the winds of change; you will break.

Find balance in this practice, too. You also should not flip your beliefs on a whim just to avoid being labeled as closed-minded. You can be open to changing your opinion without doing so every time you are prompted. Any adjustment to your opinions should be preceded by careful consideration.

Be willing to reevaluate your judgments of others. You should not jump to conclusions about others either. Do not forsake your own beliefs to force a connection with someone, but allow for the possibility that you are compatible, even if the two of you disagree. The greatest threat to the advancement of American culture is the absence of civil discourse. Increased division in the United States discourages tolerance; people are less inclined to acknowledge commonalities or to even be willing to listen to an opposing opinion. This division stifles the cooperation of intellects, and that, in turn, hinders humanity's ability to progress. To be willing to change your opinion, you must first be willing to listen and understand counter-arguments. Identify your opposition's rationale, and use that understanding as an opportunity to strengthen your opinion, either by modifying it or by learning how to better defend it.

If you are unable to be open-minded while also being steadfast in your beliefs, then you will fall short of your potential. You will not give yourself the opportunity to develop sound logic to back your own perspective, and you will forsake interactions with people whose views differ from your own. Civil discourse, disagreement, and competition are necessary for change, so they are necessary for progress because progress is positive change. Find comfort in the fact that everyone has a unique opinion, and do not discount those that do not align with your own. Take care to bolster your opinions, but also be willing to change them.

60. Change is the universal nature; it is an inescapable fact. By this, stagnation is impossible. If you are not experiencing positive progress, then you are falling behind. Entropy is both a physical and chemical property that is simply defined as a trend toward disorder. Both in the macroscopic and microscopic worlds, entities are constantly changing; the universe is constantly expanding, and every molecule is decaying. Just as it is in the physical universe, in life, change is omnipresent. To traverse life's dynamic landscape, you must recognize it as such.

Know that there is no such thing as being stagnant, for the world around you is constantly moving ahead. If you are idle, then you are moving backwards, relative to everything else. The physical world around you is always moving and changing, but there is also constant change within you. Identify how you are changing and make it positive, allowing for progress. Time stops for no one, so seize the moment by using it to change in a productive way. Being enveloped in the constant forward motion of the world and time should propel you forward, too. It should feel like your running partner is pushing you toward your personal record. That partner is the rest of the world and time itself just chugging along in the lane next to you, matching you stride for stride. Strive for self-improvement and progress. If you are not progressing, then you are falling behind.

23. Any negative reaction to your personal expression or achievement is just others' way of justifying why they did not do it themselves. This is to say that you should never be deterred from pursuing your passions or from voicing your opinions due to a fear of disapproval. If you are intrinsically motivated and passionate about something, then you can unlock your entire potential. Those who discredit your passions or refuse to acknowledge them are those who feel lost and have none of their own. Be a strong, shining example of how to openly engage with your passions, and lead others to find purpose by shamelessly pursuing theirs.

32. The Squeeze Theorem applied to life: No individual is more important than you, and you are no less important than any other individual. If you are not greater nor lesser, then you are equal. In math, the squeeze theorem describes a relationship between three functions to illustrate a property of limits. The functions are arranged such that $f(x) <= h(x) <= g(x)$ at all points. When the value of $f(x)$ and $g(x)$ are equal, you know that $h(x)$ also shares that value. The two

outer functions—one lesser than h(x) and one greater than it—squeeze together, and all three unite at a single point.

People perceive others to be greater or lesser than them, according to arbitrary metrics such as education level, economic or social status, income, etc. Those metrics are irrelevant to an individual's intellectual or emotional capacity, and they do not determine the caliber of one's character. In accordance with this graphical analogy, f(x) represents those perceived to be lesser, and g(x) represents those perceived to be greater. Allow those functions to squeeze together, eliminating any difference between them. Draw back g(x) and lift f(x) so that they both intersect with h(x) at single point. That point reflects the equality of humanity. Live where all three graphs intersect, for that is reality. All of humanity has shared, intrinsic value that is equal for all people, and you are no exception.

What does equality look like? It is when no one views themselves as greater or lesser than any other person and treats themselves and others as such. That is a definition of equality that is actionable. The notion of equality is only that, a notion, unless you actively treat everyone (including yourself) with equal respect and value.

33. Privilege should not be met with guilt but rather with inherent ambition and a sense of responsibility to better the world. First, it is a privilege to be alive, and it is a privilege to be alive at this point in human history. The privilege of life should not be taken for granted, as life itself brings limitless possibilities and potential. Throughout life, however, privilege can differ. A discrepancy in

privilege arises from the fact that people are presented with different circumstances, starting points, and experiences. There are advantages in regard to attaining opportunity, flexibility, and mobility that are not equally distributed (unlike the privilege of life, which is given to all).

Privilege impacts the probability of success and prosperity, but it does not affect the possibility of success. To think of it another way, an advantageous starting point in life does not guarantee success, but it often provides a higher quantity of opportunity. The opportunities that are available to you are completely and uniquely within your control. It is each person's responsibility to capitalize on opportunities and work to provide others with a higher quantity of them. Anyone can do that for anyone else, regardless of their level of privilege; it is solely dependent on effort.

If you are better-off, do not apologize for it. Instead, use your good fortune in life to do even more for the rest of the world and for yourself. If you are fortunate enough to have excess opportunity, then work to provide opportunities for others. No one has an excuse for why they cannot improve their quality of life to some degree. Privilege merely allows for more opportunities to do so. Seek opportunities and seize each that you are granted. Work to create opportunities for others as well as for yourself, and never become immobilized by guilt, self-pity, or a perceived inability to better your situation. The severity of struggle varies just as fortune and privilege vary, but everyone has struggles, and everyone has opportunities. Regardless of your level of privilege, strive be someone who overcomes struggles by relentlessly pursuing your goals with constant confidence that you will achieve them.

66. The macro is made in the micro; there is a process in everything, and a desirable outcome cannot be reached without complete effort throughout the process. Focus on constantly achieving incremental progress. Instantaneous mastery should not be the metric for success, for to truly master anything, you must engage in a journey of learning. There are no shortcuts when it comes to attaining your goals in their fullest form. Your focus in any moment should be just that: in the moment. Be aware of the macro, for it helps to orient your goals in the present, but actively live in the micro. Enjoy the experience of each learning journey and realize that taking shortcuts only causes you to forsake potentially enriching experiences.

The micro includes individual decisions and experiences where the macro is the sum of the micro. Each new moment is the sum of past experiences. You may regret forsaking an experience in the past that could have been beneficial in shaping the present. A moment in the future is the sum of past experiences, including those in the present. That should be reassuring because it means that you have the power to shape your experience in each moment and shape your future. If every step toward the future is enriching and enjoyable, then the future that arrives will be purposeful and fulfilling.

To craft this idyllic future, identify your passions and use them to inform your decisions, for passion is the mother of purpose.

Decisions determine your experience, and if you decide to follow your passions, then you will arrive at purpose. If you constantly pursue your passions, you will be living your purpose before even discovering what it is. Understand the dependency that the micro and macro have on each other; the only way to achieve purpose in the macro is to pursue your passions in the micro.

36. Events and actions in the past are what determine the present, but you, in the now, determine the future. Continuously be mindful of your power to enact change and dictate your own actions. Embrace the present, for that is the only way to command the future.

39. Know that you are worthy of being heard, of being wherever you are or aspire to be, and of belonging wherever you may be. Own it, and no one will question your place. Each moment is cumulative; the present is dependent on the past, so any and all points in life are dependent on your prior actions. In accordance with that idea, the state of the present is what it should be, so embrace it. You are where you are meant to be. Others may question the validity of your position, your qualifications, or your credibility, but you should not question yourself. Be reassured and reminded of your potential and of the validity of your contributions. Find a sense of complete belonging because you belong in the present. Whatever the present brings is what you are meant to receive from it, for the present was forged from the past. If you, in fact, do not want to be where you are, you should still not reject or deny it. Instead, act now to change it. The past may have brought about an undesirable

present, but you can make adjustments now in order to arrive at a desirable future.

98. The human experience is defined by ups and downs, and *a* human's experience is defined by their response to those extremes. Sorrow is inevitable, but negative experiences are beneficial because they help fuel your desire to achieve happiness. Humanity is unified in the common truth that no one is immune to emotion. It is those who are able to monitor and dictate their reactions who are emotionally strong. Temper the effect that external forces have on your disposition to achieve higher clarity of thought and increased control of your emotions. Life will deliver both boosts and blows; it is unavoidable. Do not let the boosts lift you so high that it hurts to fall, and do not let the blows burry you so deep that you cannot resurface.

The most important skill in achieving a balanced disposition and emotional strength is the ability to identify and address your emotions. Strength does not come from shielding yourself from emotion altogether; dodging emotions only leads you to internalize them. Eventually, those internalized emotions will surface and result in a negatively-fueled catharsis. Continually address emotions so that there is never a stockpile of emotion that seems insurmountable.

Your emotions are like waves that oscillate between peaks and valleys, but you can control the heights of those peaks and the depths of those valleys. Positivity and logic will allow you to temper emotional extremes. On the negative extreme, use positivity to conjure hope and combat sorrow. On the positive extreme, employ logic to ground your euphoria in reality. Recognize what is within your control, and ensure that your emotions are not governed by events that are out of your control. Determine your reactions and perception; wield emotions as a tool for personal development.

26. The more constants there are, the more comfortable and stress-free life will be. Try to limit uncertainty in your daily actions by establishing routines and increasing your overall efficiency. This ability is important, as there is constant movement and change in day-to-day life. Make sure to be completely prepared for what you expect to happen so that you can more effectively adapt to the unexpected.

Routines are valuable if they are purposeful and do not impose monotony. A routine is like a loop; there are a set of actions that must all be completed within that loop. Picture traversing this loop as you would drive around the block in a car. The quickest way to drive in a square is to make four right turns because, with each action that you take, you are moving with the flow of traffic. You do not maximize efficiency by going about it the other way—using left turns—because you would have to yield to traffic. The same mindset can be applied to routines. If you formulate consistent, familiar sets of actions, then you do not have to yield to heavy traffic in your mind. There is little consideration or planning needed for routines because of the familiarity and autonomy of them. Routines are beneficial in the long run because they increase efficiency and productivity. By consistently creating simple routines, you can develop a habit of finding the most efficient method for many sets of actions. It is beneficial to be in the habit of seeking out efficiency because efficiency is objectively desirable.

10. Being stressed is a choice that is determined by your outlook, so find a positive outlook that allows you to accomplish your work while not feeling stressed or weighed down by it. Colloquially, stress is used in a negative context, and it is often related to mental strain and anxiety. A distinction must be made, though, between stress and urgency. Urgency and stress can both act as motivational forces, but stress is an entirely negative entity that directly opposes confidence and, therefore, hinders your ability to perform. Urgency can be wielded as a positive force for progress. Feelings of urgency are often unavoidable, but they can certainly be productive. Stress can be avoided; you can choose to negate the negative mindset that stress incurs. Urgency and stress are often incited by deadlines or by a full to-do-list, and both emotions urge you to make progress to relieve that pressure. However, stress is a hindrance to the mind; even though you want to make progress to alleviate pressure, stress restricts your ability to do so. Contrarily, urgency serves as an unencumbering accelerant. When faced with a potentially stressful situation, lean into urgency and couple it with confidence as you work to tackle each task. Urgency is rooted externally; it pulls you toward progress. Stress takes an internal toll and often immobilizes you, clouding the mind and damaging confidence. Choose to be urgent, not stressed. Propel yourself forward and refuse to endure self-imposed negativity.

85. Saturate your experiences with your attention so that you forge more vivid memories. Though it may seem that memory is a purely mechanical and involuntary function of the mind, constant and complete engagement with your experiences can help strengthen your memory. It is detrimental and inefficient to act without being fully present, for it dilutes the potential impact of your actions. The impact of a single experience endures in memory, for memory houses the legacy of your experiences. The longer and more clearly you remember something, the greater its legacy. A lack of focus weakens the moment at hand and limits the possibility for that experience to have lasting benefits in memory. Your most impactful experiences should be the ones whose legacies you want to preserve in memory. If you further the legacy of an experience by giving it your attention, then you can continually learn from it and call upon it from memory. Be attentive in each moment to ensure that the legacies of your experiences are full and lasting.

Instead of puttering along through your day in idle, stand attentively at the helm, and consciously navigate that which comes your way. Take note of how experiences influence your heading. Regarding your level of attention, treat every experience as if it were new and unfamiliar. With new experiences, the mind takes an involuntary pause so that the impact of that experience is realized and remembered. Take new places, for example. You can likely picture a place that you have been only once just as well as you could picture your own bedroom. Novel experiences are often the easiest to remember, so treat every experience as such, for every experience is unique. The setting you are in, the company you have, the actions you take, the idea at hand, and the emotions you feel are all factors that differentiate one experience from the next. Pay mind to each of those factors in order to recognize the novelty in each experience and cement moments in memory. Each instance of an experience brings about a new combination of those factors, and, therefore, can occupy a new, unique place in your memory. Voluntarily take pause to absorb experiences so that you may forge their legacies in long-lasting memories and utilize their impact.

29. Philosophers do not sit on the beach, peering from the shore. They climb a mountain to gaze upon all that leads to the shore and the entire sea beyond. A philosopher is synonymous with a thinker that ponders both the nature of the world and the nature of themselves. It is a thinker that is motivated to do so out of a pure desire to acquire knowledge. Learning is entirely beneficial, so exert the effort that is needed to attain new knowledge; climb the mountain. There is always more to see; the more you learn, the more you discover what there is to know. Similarly, climbing a mountain reveals so much more of your surroundings than what you would see from the shore.

Conscious effort is needed to elevate your thoughts and differentiate your pursuit of knowledge from others'. Consider mountains and physical elevation. You must exert effort and energy to summit a mountain, and that is why not everyone will do it, but there is immense value to reap from such an endeavor. That value comes from the opportunity to attain a new perspective. You can facilitate your own intellectual exploration by deciding to make the climb. Planting your footprints on untouched terrain is the most vivid illustration of expanding your boundaries and broadening your horizons. Strive to do that with both physical and intellectual exploration. You can differentiate yourself by adopting a mindset that promotes constant exploration and the pursuit of knowledge. Your knowledge of the world is dependent on what you have experienced, and the breadth of your experience is dependent on your willingness to venture into the unknown. Pursue an exhaustive perspective by acquiring knowledge about yourself and about the world around you. Every mind has the inherent potential and inclination to inquire and to wonder. Give in to the temptation of curiosity.

46. Never become numb to change, yet accept it as part of nature. Being numb to change means that you have no appropriate response to it because you have no reaction at all. Instead, know that change is inevitable. That mindset will ensure that you are prepared to respond to change in a productive way. Ignoring change or trying to avoid it will cause you to fall behind, consuming precious energy that could have been used to promote positive change, or progress.

27. Acknowledge a need for change, progress, reform etc., but be conscious and reminded of the positive aspects of each situation. If it is difficult to identify positivity in something, look either to the intentions or to the potential of the matter at hand. A beneficial result is always either intended or attainable. If there were no good intentions behind a given pursuit, then that course of action can be pivoted to serve for good. If there were good intentions but

nothing good has come yet, then enact reform. Acknowledge the potential for good, beneficial results, and propose change that helps achieve those results. There is always the potential for a positive outcome.

97. Pain should act as a catalyst. If you allow pain to become injury, it, instead, hinders progress. Whether it is emotional or physical in nature, pain is not intrinsically harmful. Pain, in some form or another, is necessary for progress. Only the mind and your perception of pain can turn pain into injury.

Bodily injury impedes your physical abilities and hinders progress. The human body has abilities that stretch far beyond the parameters set by the mind. Often, the mind sets parameters for your body that are based on pain, not injury. Take control of these mental barriers to action. If you allow yourself to endure pain, then it will be less painful in the future. Prove to your mind that your body can go further. What may be painful once is often never painful again because you have extended the boundaries of your abilities and of your tolerance.

Apply this principle for emotional troubles, too; use pain to fuel change and adaptation. You should not be deterred by painful failures, but motivated. Alleviate that pain by creating more positive emotional experiences in the future. Emotional injury is most often manifested in a reduction in self-confidence or self-image, which could be caused by being hurt in a relationship or by others' opinions. It is natural and acceptable for those experiences to cause pain, but do not let them cause injury by damaging your self-image or your long-term mental state.

Pain may be involuntary, but you control the severity of its physical and emotion effects. Repurpose negative experiences by allowing them to strengthen your resolve and tolerance.

37. At any instant, you only have control of what happens in a moment of time and in a sliver of space, but the sum of those instants yields your experience and impact. You can control your mental state as well as your actions. Know that you have been given the freedom to act in your space at this time. Focus on what you do in each sliver of time and space so that you make the most of each. Recognize which of those moments bring you the most joy, comfort, enrichment, and overall fulfillment so that you may constantly pursue positive experiences. Be equally aware of your effect on the world as you are of its effect on you. If you constantly engage in this sort of evaluation, then you can pivot your actions, when necessary, to ensure that your impact is positive and that you are being positively impacted by the world around you.

79. Do not work to become famous. Become famous for your work. Working to become famous means that your primary motivation is to be recognized by others. A focus on external validation only limits your potential impact, for it draws nearer the horizons of your individuality. Use others' feedback to inform your decisions and actions, but do not work for the approval of the masses. Act to fulfill your own goals, and be satisfied with internal validation, for it is often the only validation you will get. If you are

confident in your convictions, morals, and aptitude, then you should need only your own approval.

If you do, indeed, establish sound motivations and are independently pursuing your own passions, then you will be recognized for it. You will stand out. Most people long for others' validation. If you truly long for nothing else but your own approval and satisfaction, then you will break off from the herd. Become a leader just by following your own passions and furthering your ideas. Aim to better the rest of the world; do not merely appeal to it. If you are genuinely motivated to better yourself and the world around you, then you will be recognized for doing so.

30. Your name will only be recorded in history if you act to impact the future. Your focus should be grounded in the present, but do consider the past and the future. The only way to know how to positively impact the future is by learning from the past.

Do not hold excessive admiration for historical figures to the point where you are distracted from your own pursuits. You should never be envious of others' accomplishments. To be envious is to accept that you are incapable of ever accomplishing the same as someone else; you would not be jealous of something that you know you could do yourself. Envy detracts from your potential and grounds your thoughts in the past.

Just as you should not allow envy to draw your focus away from the present, you should not be transfixed on the future. Even if you are certain that you will succeed, there should be no reason that you desire to rush to that end. Such a desire will lead to mistakes and miscalculations in the present that may dissolve the prosperous future you had conceived. Consider the ramifications of each action and estimate those ramifications by using knowledge from the past. Do not envy history. If you create history now, you will become part of it in the future.

93. Live in a time that is balanced between your past and future. Do not long for the past but be willing to relive it. Do not rush to the future but be sure to enjoy it when it comes. To be willing to relive the past, you must not resent it. You should not resent the past, for it has brought you the present. If you are dissatisfied with the present, know that you have the power to change it. Desirable changes can only come through incremental progress and conscious effort in each moment.

41. Maximize efficiency. Define what efficiency is to you, and know that it is dependent on both quality and quantity. Coordinate your actions and processes accordingly. Whatever your goals are, you should strive to achieve them efficiently so that you have the opportunity to engage in all of your interests. Do not speed through the process of any pursuit; that is false efficiency, for efficiency demands quality—not just quantity. Maximizing efficiency is essential if you are to reach your potential. Given that you have benevolent intentions to better yourself and the world around you, maximizing your efficiency is then synonymous with imparting your maximum positive impact on the world. Employ efficiency in daily activities as well as in your pursuits of long-term goals. You will achieve a higher

quantity of your goals and have the opportunity to pursue higher-quality goals in the future.

40. Prioritize quality over quantity. Realize that in some instances, though, the highest level of quality is achieved by the most efficient route to quantity. Where there may seem to be only the pursuit of quantity, know that there is a scalable quality to that pursuit.

For example, the goal of picking up tennis balls is to get all the balls back in the basket so that you can keep playing. That is a pursuit of quantity. However, there are objectively better ways to pick up tennis balls than to do so one at a time, for instance. The way to distinguish the "better" of two ways to pick up tennis balls is by comparing the efficiency of the methodologies. Since quality is an inherent factor in efficiency, it is also inherent to any pursuit of quantity. Quality, in such a pursuit, refers to the methodology used to achieve quantity. A flawed methodology would not efficiently deliver quantity, and, therefore, it lacks quality.

80. Death is but an instant in the eternal breath of your life and legacy. Everyone longs for profound, significant experiences, for those can greatly alter the course of life. However, these special experiences are difficult to recognize in the moment; you must reflect on them in order to realize their significance.

Take the experience of attending a funeral. What may consume your thoughts, in the moment, is questions of why death came then or why it came for that person. You may think back to conversations that you had or experiences that you shared during their life. In the moment, your thoughts are probably consumed by the idea of death, but death is a single, isolated, inevitable event. Death is an instant, and life is eternal. Death is not an ending. If you consider it graphically, death would be merely a removable discontinuity in the graph of life—a hole in the otherwise continuous function. That function has an unbounded domain that begins at the start of life and extends for eternity. Preceding death is your experience and the impact that you impart during life. After death, your legacy takes over, and those that you impacted carry it forth forever.

Your legacy extends the impact of your life. During the finite interval of time that is within your control, maximize your positive impact. Your legacy will be strengthened as a result. Seize the finite amount of time that you are allotted by furthering your positive impact, and act in the present so that the future may be better for it.

47. The best time in life is now. There is no other time than right now in which you have agency over outcome; the past is fixed, and the future is dependent on the present. Why would you prefer any time other than one that has infinite potential and endless, but malleable outcomes?

If you are to ever feel satisfied or happy, it is essential to believe that the best time in your life is right now. If you would say that you wish to revert to college, your childhood, or some other time of your life, that reflects poorly on your actions in the present. Do more to work toward your goals and in pursuit of your passions. Recognize the source of your dissatisfaction and, in each moment, work to remedy it. Start with changing your mindset by acknowledge your ability to respond to your desires and engage with your passions.

Then, after adopting a mindset that gives you agency over your life, act to make it a desirable one. The power of the present is that it allows you to redefine the future by using knowledge from the past. In no other time in your life are you as empowered as you are right now because you have the freedom to act and, in turn, the freedom to enact change. There is responsibility and accountability that accompany this power because all actions yield consequences. Once you experience them, though, consequences can be a source of new knowledge that you glean from the past. Pursue knowledge to inform how you should act now in order to shape a desirable future.

CONFIDENCE: FUEL FOR THE MIND

43. *Be devout in your own greatness.*

A high level of self-confidence is essential to achieving your potential and to living the life you desire. To be truly confident, you must recognize your own greatness and acknowledge that you have an infinite capacity for it. Just the fact that you can control your thoughts and actions is enough to be great. That is greatness derived from the ability to enact change. How much change? Well, there is no limit to the potential ramifications of your actions. To be confident is to take stake in yourself—to invest in yourself. Would you really prefer to bet against yourself? Would you short your own company's stock? Just take the leap, and be confident. It will bolster your individuality and improve the quality of your interactions. Foster self-confidence and lead by example; help others realize their own greatness by demonstrating self-confidence and assuring them of their merit and their capabilities. Encourage others to never waiver from certainty in their capabilities, and believe that you, too, have the potential to accomplish anything.

Even though confidence can be faked or flipped on in a moment, genuine self-confidence must be cultivated over time. Confidence comes from experiences of feeling unsure and uncomfortable yet still succeeding. You will learn that you have every reason to believe in yourself. Apply that belief in the form of confidence.

In every aspect of life and in each endeavor, your confidence zone should exceed your comfort zone. Most people find comfort in familiar places and in doing that at which they know they can succeed. Your comfort zone includes only the actions that you believe have the highest chance of success. Discomfort, on the other hand, stems from uncertainty and risk. The level of risk that you perceive can be altered by your level of confidence. Perception determines reality, so you can either convince yourself to be unsure or convince yourself to be completely certain, solely based on your perception. You can redefine your comfort zone by increasing your level of confidence. Confidence is the belief that you are capable of alleviating risk and increasing the likelihood of success. To increase self-confidence is to reduce the uncertainty and perceived risk of your actions.

If your comfort zone consists of everything that you are certain you will succeed in doing, then anything within your comfort zone should be done with confidence. By approaching your comfort zone with complete confidence, you will more quickly become comfortable doing new things. There should be nothing on the border of what you perceive to be your limits of comfort that is not within your confidence zone.

The essential part of managing your confidence and comfort is that you must always be confident beyond where you are comfortable. If this is not the case, then your comfort zone will never grow. However, your confidence zone should not dwarf your comfort zone, for that is hubris. Always prioritize confidence over comfort, but temper confidence with prudence to ensure that you do not blindly take action.

In order to extend your comfort zone, you must venture to the edge of it. Use confidence as a companion as you seek discomfort. By wielding confidence against uncertainty and the unknown, you will extend the breadth of your experience, gain knowledge about yourself and the world around you, and approach your potential. You have an infinite capacity for thought and growth that cannot be fully realized without self-confidence. If you are more inclined to feel confident than comfortable, you will be able to be uncomfortable and uncertain, yet still confident. Confidence, if extended beyond your comfort zone, has the power to reduce discomfort and eliminate barriers to action.

13. The key to confidence is the ability to justify your actions and opinions with your own beliefs, experiences, and logic; it comes from knowing yourself and never wavering from your principles. If

you continuously adhere to principles that you have determined, then you will not be burdened by uncertainty. You need certainty to act confidently, and the best way to achieve certainty is by establishing morals, values, and expectations for yourself. Expend the necessary time and effort to truly and accurately identify your principles, for that is the path to clarity. You need confidence to grow your comfort zone, and confidence is bred from having clarity in regard to your actions.

90. The fuel for your actions should come from within, not from recognition or external validation. It is admirable to act for the sake of others, but when you act for the sake of others' approval—merely to receive recognition—you are indulging in selfish and unproductive desires. In aiming for validation, you may succeed in appeasing others, but you will forsake your own nature. Your ideals, beliefs, and convictions should remain steady and consistent, despite the dynamic situations to which they are applied. Regardless of variable conditions, your morality must not allow for exceptions. Adhere to your principles even in the absence of an observer or without the threat of evaluation. Others' opinions of you should not determine the caliber or the nature of your actions. Immoral influences should not deter you, and you should need no encouragement to employ good morals. Do not seek external validation. Instead, ensure that your actions are congruent with your principles, and you will possess genuine integrity.

94. Long to be held accountable. The only people who wish to be held accountable for their actions are those who act according

to their nature—those who never deviate from their principles. No one wants to be associated with actions that they regret. An action is regrettable if you would not want it to contribute to your identity. By constantly adhering to your morals and principles, you will limit these sorts of actions.

Someone who is proud of the way that they conduct themselves does not shy away from accepting accountability, and they do not see it as burden. Be confident in your convictions so that you may openly accept association with and accountability for your actions. Even in the aftermath of a mistake, take ownership of your decisions, and address the consequences. Those who dissociate themselves from their actions after making a mistake merely shift the blame and formulate excuses. In this process of evasion, they rob themselves of the opportunity to refine their decision-making abilities and rethink their motives, methods, and priorities. Surety, commitment, and ownership will allow you openly accept accountability.

16. Do not exude false confidence regarding a matter of which you lack knowledge. Doing so is a form of dishonesty, for people will believe what you say if it is said with confidence. Admitting a lack of knowledge is just as important as possessing and articulating knowledge. The influence that confidence has on people's perceptions is staggering. This, in many ways, is a positive effect of confidence, for it empowers individuals to inspire others. However, the influence of confidence, used in conjunction with invalidity, results in manipulation.

Presenting something as a fact, even though you are unsure of it, is not beneficial to you nor to your audience. No one will learn anything of true meaning. In a social scenario, do not disguise falsehoods as facts for the purpose of joining in on a conversation. If you heard a rumor, do not fill in the gaps of the story and recount it as if you were a firsthand witness. The fact is that you are unsure of the whole truth, so let that be known to your audience. This is an example of incomplete knowledge, but there is a distinction to be made between incomplete knowledge and limited experience.

You should never use confidence as a guise when you lack knowledge of objective facts. When you lack experience, though, leverage confidence as means of approaching a new endeavor. Confidence should not be used to gain approval or external validation, but it should be used to combat fear, uncertainty, or nervousness. If you were to give a speech and had little experience doing so, exuding false confidence can help you succeed. In settings where you lack experience, do not fake it until you make it. Instead, fake it only until you start it. False confidence quickly becomes genuine confidence; you need only to fake confidence until the gun fires at the starting block. Once you have begun, genuine confidence will surface, and success will seem much more attainable. The fact that you had the courage to attempt the race will give you confidence, fueling a belief in your abilities.

Employing momentary false confidence is often the only way to be confident outside your comfort zone. False confidence is not misleading or manipulative as long as you do not present falsehoods as facts. When you lack experience, faking it until you start will allow you to approach the task at hand. Do not drag objective facts from certainty into the realm of ambiguity by misusing false confidence. Utilize fleeting bursts of false confidence to expand your own realms of comfort and possibility.

57. Fears of death preserve life, but fears of living inhibit it. Fear death—the end of life—because death is final. In death, there cannot be change, and there cannot be progress. On the direct contrary is life, which is pure, unlimited potential. Be empowered, not crippled, by the opportunity of life. Do not fear any part of life, for that would serve to dilute living. The only fears that you should allow yourself to indulge in are fears that preserve life by deterring actions that would endanger it. As long as life is preserved, there is nothing to fear, because life is a source of boundless potential and unrelenting hope. Death is the only thing that can eliminate hope, for it eliminates the potential for change. Fears of life inhibit living, but fears of death preserve hope and opportunity.

Inhibitors—fears that restrict life—are the speed limit of progress. They prohibit exploration by fortifying the boundary of your comfort zone. Fears of living lock up some of life's infinite potential. Eliminate inhibiting fears and unlock that potential; weaken the boundaries of your comfort zone. If fear confines you to your comfort zone, then progress will stagnate, for progress is predicated on new experiences. There are very few new experiences that lie within your comfort zone, and your volume of new experiences is restricted by inhibitors. These fears, therefore, restrict your exposure to new hobbies, relationships, unrealized talents, etc. Be comforted by the immense potential in living life freely and expanding your comfort zone. Do not let that potential be captured by unnecessary fears. Unlock new potential by being confident and fearless in the pursuit of new experiences.

Seizing your chance at life involves alleviating fears that detract from it. All fears detract from living except the fear death. You can eliminate those unproductive, restrictive fears in the following two ways: (1) recognize inhibiting fears as irrational and use pure reason to deflate them; or (2) weigh the opportunity cost of your fear and convince yourself that you would be better-off if you were to overcome it. Either method could be used independently, or the two could be used together. Employ these tactics so that you never view an inhibiting fear as rational or beneficial.

If you do find yourself wanting to rationalize a given fear, you must critically consider how life would be without it. If you can reasonably determine that life would be more dangerous and less enjoyable if you were to alleviate that fear, then maybe it is, in fact, a preservative fear. In that case, you should allow that fear to remain. Only after this sort of consideration and analysis can you determine the validity of a fear and deem a it rational.

One intrinsically and universally restrictive fear is a fear of the unknown. That fear, by its nature, restricts exploration, for exploration involves ventures into unknown territory. The fear of death is an exception to this rule because death is an eternal unknown—an unanswerable question. While it is certain that death will occur, the nature of death and what follows it are unknown. They are unknowns that will be never be addressed in life, for they can only be understood by experiencing death.

Death is the only unknown you should fear, for there is nothing to gain from exploring death. However, all other expeditions into the unknown have the potential to provide new insights, enriching experiences, and life-altering relationships. Expose yourself to new territory so that you more frequently have new experiences and are able to expand your comfort zone. Venture toward and welcome in new experiences. By doing so, you will more accurately recognize inhibiting fears and be able to dispatch them. Only allow preservative fears to prevail in your mind so that you can unlock all of life's potential.

22. Courage is uncommon, and witnessing courage increases motivation and self-confidence. The capacity for courage is omnipresent and inherent in everyone, but acts of courage are more rare. Courage is the capacity to surmount adversity, and courageous actions are individual's attempts to do so. Acts of courage are so rare because they require you to take a leap of faith and lunge toward some challenge, but no one is naturally inclined to seek difficulty and risk. There is a natural aversion to difficulty because of the responsibility and effort associated with it. There must be a logical reason for one elect to increase risk or difficulty. A valid and common reason to do so is that life is better on the other side of adversity—on the other side of fear. You are capable of surmounting adversity and you, as well as those around you, will be better for it.

You must prioritize long term benefits over short term discomfort and difficulty; that is necessary if you hope to be courageous. Adversity implies short-term pain, but also the potential for long-term gain.

The primary benefit of courage is that it can broaden your horizons; it can expand your comfort zone. Courage lies between what you are willing to do and that which you are comfortable doing—it is your confidence zone minus your comfort zone. You cannot be courageous within your comfort zone because, within your comfort zone, there is no adversity to face. If you are only confident within your comfort zone, then you are only willing to take action when you know that you can succeed. There is no courage in that.

Courage is what allows you to extend your comfort zone, but not before you become confident in uncharted territory—in uncomfortable situations. Courage is confidence less comfort. Become confident beyond what you are comfortable with, and you will increase your capacity for courage.

Focus on acting courageously, near the limits of your confidence, so that you may extend your comfort zone and more easily find success in a wider range of actions. The more that you are comfortable doing, the easier it is to grow, but to grow, you must be courageous. Consider again the idea that courage is confidence less comfort and think of the experience of jumping off a diving board. The first time you do it, you may consider jumping to be a courageous act. What about the second time? Did it take the same amount of courage to jump in, or were you more comfortable doing it the second time? If your comfort level increased and your confidence stayed the same, then it was less courageous to jump the second time. Maybe your confidence did change, though. Maybe you now think that you can dive in head first off of the board. That is growth. That is progress, brought forth by courage. Do not settle for shyly stepping off the diving board into the water. Do a swan dive, do a flip, and expand your comfort zone with each new increase in confidence and each new implementation of courage.

  Literal leaps of faith are not the only manifestations of courage. Do not solely measure your level of courage or your progress with it by how often you take physical risks. Separate physical courage from moral courage. Physical courage is predicated mostly on instinct or bravery and involves physical risk, whereas moral courage is the capacity to adhere to your principles and morals. Physical courage is less accessible, for a specific scenario must align to even allow for it to surface; you cannot and stop a thief if you never witness a robbery in progress. Moral courage should be your focus, for it is constantly and universally accessible. You can consciously develop it, and there are infinite opportunities to employ it in life. You may never see a robbery in progress to disrupt with an act of physical courage, but you always have the decision whether to be the thief, yourself. That is how you employ moral courage: by always choosing to not be the thief and constantly adhering to your morals. Strengthen and cultivate your character with moral courage as you would use physical courage to expand your comfort zone. If you more often act with confidence, then you are more capable of being courageous.

18. Having confidence in your abilities is the first step toward success, and the truest form of confidence results from preparation and practice. Prepare by clearly defining your belief system and practice those principles by constantly considering and acting in accordance with them. Test the validity of your principles by employing them, and if you deem them to be flawed, pivot your perspective.

If you are able to identify your beliefs and values independently and not be influenced by others, then you can truly understand your nature and start becoming comfortable with who you are. In the processes of education and childhood development, you first learn now to interact with the world and understand the nature of it. After that, you are expected to know how to act in the world that you have come to understand. Your understanding of the world and your behavior within it will certainly differ from anyone else's. The path to establishing and articulating a unique perspective can involve many periods of uncertainty and discouraging unknowns. To traverse these periods effectively, identify your values, principles, and morals. Know how you want to act and constantly adhere to that ideal, but be willing to pivot your perspective if you deem it necessary. To live and act within a self-defined framework will give you more surety, increasing confidence through preparation and practice.

54. People are interested in what you have to say and if they are not, they will be once you say it. Know that your ideas are worth being heard and never shy away from voicing your thoughts. If you are passionate or knowledgeable about a subject, then there is no reason to avoid discussing it. Have confidence in your ability to articulate your ideas, and do so willingly and frequently. If you feel that your skills of self-expression and articulation are lacking, know that the only way to improve them is to practice. Still, then, the answer is to express yourself and share your ideas. Compel others with your speech and garner their attention if they do not willingly grant it outright.

When you are the listener, let people know that you are interested in their opinions. Be forthcoming with your attention, and give genuine consideration to the insights of others, for they may positively influence your perspective. Nothing and no one but you should determine your opinions. However, opening your mind to outside ideas will make your opinions more tested and refined. The more you consider the validity of your own perspective, the more chances you will have to pivot it and improve your reasoning for it. Be open to others' ideas and give due consideration to them.

You should be confident enough in your own thoughts to share them with others. Some people will attempt to stifle your opinions in order to bolster their own, but you should not act as such. Give others the chance to consider your ideas, and maybe you will cause them to pivot *their* perspective. Ideas are products of the mind, but compelling ideas are products of speech; the impact of compelling ideas is lost if they are not shared. Make yourself heard, and people will long to hear more from you.

82. Encourage the successes of others; resenting their success will tempt the creation of excuses or a lack of self-confidence. This resentment arises when you witness others' successes and do not believe that you could achieve the same level of success. Everyone's accomplishments should be encouraged because human progress is driven by the ambitions, innovations, and creations of individuals. If you are averse to the successes of others, then you are averse to the human progress, for human progress is the aggregate of individual successes. Witnessing others' accomplishments and their receipt of accolades should motivate you, not discourage you. Jealousy has no place in the mind of a confident individual. A confident person is, instead, focused on their own pursuits and certain that they will reach their goals.

86. Do not change yourself, find yourself. Everyone has the capacity to be benevolent and to achieve their potential. If you feel lost, do not look without to decide how to act; you should, instead, strive to identify your intrinsic nature. You are unique and independent from any other person, so do not look elsewhere to define what is within you.

You have the capacity to become the person that you want to be, largely due to confidence, for it opens the door to possibility. Without confidence, there is little hope for personal development. Once you indulge in self-confidence, you become more capable of accomplishing your goals. Then, each stride toward your goals bolsters your confidence. It is a reciprocal relationship; confidence breeds progress, and progress breeds confidence. Cultivate self-confidence, and then allow progress and success to further extend your confidence. Find confidence in the fact that you are who you are supposed to be. If you feel lost, you have just not yet found yourself.

75. In spite of resistance, redirect current to illuminate a bulb that shines brighter than the rest. There is always resistance to the expression of individuality because many people are unsure of how to accomplish that in their own lives. Do not shy away from your passions; accept your true nature. This resistance to individuality often motivates people to revert to the norm. Subscribing to a group mentality, or following the herd, negatively affects your potential because you are sacrificing individuality for comfort. If you are able to, instead, resist a pull toward the norm and stay your course, you will have the opportunity to fulfill your potential. Picture a set of lightbulbs in a circuit. The brightest bulbs are those with the highest resistance. Like those brighter bulbs, resist the urge to fall in line and join the masses; refuse to revert to the norm. Be steadfast in your beliefs, shamelessly pursue your passions, and become the bulb that outshines the rest, despite the resistance it requires to do so.

CHARACTER: YOUR INTERNAL ROADMAP

9. Respect the game; no excuses.

Everyone is a cartographer when it comes to life. No one knows the way, and everyone's journey is different. You can ask for directions, but you must always decide whether or not to follow them. Character, or your internal roadmap, is constructed by the decisions you make and by the moral structure you apply to life. Just like a map that models geography, your character is discovered, not invented. It is possible to incorrectly define your own character, but those missteps are just part of the process of discovery. If you do not want your roadmap to lead you astray, you must ensure that it is accurate and aligned with your moral compass. If you ever realize that you are off-course, you must not blame anything or anyone else, and look inward. It is difficult to discover your direction when you refuse accountability or deny reality, so never make excuses.

You may have heard the phrase "respect the game" in sports—maybe in little league baseball. The striking part of this mantra is that is has innumerable applications. What does it mean to respect the game of life? Try to answer that question, for it will help you establish distinct ethical boundaries and traverse ambiguous moral territory. It is essential to establish ethical boundaries in the process of "character cartography." Identify unwavering guidelines—your rules for the game—in order to confidently focus the direction of your actions. Those guidelines will act as the foundation of your character—the borders of your internal roadmap.

If you are to create a roadmap that accurately models your character, you must consciously engage in character cartography. Consider new experiences as new frontiers and define them in the context of your map. There are so many opportunities to enrich yourself, so be sure to recognize them when they come along. Pay mind to the deeper applications of your experiences, but do not let your focus be drawn away from the moment at hand. It is best to reflect on experiences with a big-picture lens in retrospect, rather than to apply that lens in real time. Make the most of each moment, but later, reflect on those moments in search of guidance for your future actions.

Character growth can come from any experience or engagement, but one example is sports and competition. The phrase "respect the game" is linked to sports, but you can take its applications further to aid in the development of your character. In sports, respecting the game means to play with good sportsmanship, to understand and adhere to the rules, and to extend respect to your teammates and opponents alike. The game of life can be seen to mirror sports in the sense that the same sort of respect should be applied to each.

In life, show respect to both friends and foes, and act with an understanding of the consequences of your actions. Baseball, for instance, can seem like an individual sport; it is easy to become concerned with only your individual performance. You may be solely concerned with your batting average or the amount of errors you have made rather than focusing on your overall contribution to the team. This self-centric view is natural and prevalent in life too, for everyone is the protagonist of their own story. Instead, try to view your performance as a contribution to a team—to humanity. Think of your actions as a part of the aggregate of human action and your morality as influencing a universal ethical code. That shift in mindset can frame your decisions in new importance, opening your mind to new possibilities.

Support your friends and family as you would your teammates and respect the efforts of your competitors. Each interaction in life is like an at-bat or an inning in the field; it is your chance to make a contribution. Prioritize the practice of making positive contributions. Live for yourself while, simultaneously, living for others. There is no need to make a compromise between your individual performance and that of the team. If you are motivated to contribute to the common good, then you will enrich yourself while doing so. Each of your actions contributes to the whole of human progress, so do not hinder that progress with immoral actions, disrespect, or a generally flawed character. Establish your character as one that promotes positive contributions to progress and one that enriches yourself and the world around you.

48. Achieve autonomous motivation for unified progress. Responding to external motivation is a nuanced skill. You must identify which influences are positive, which are negative, and then decide how to act in response to them. External influences should serve only to shape your perception, not to guide your actions. If you only act in response to external motivation, you will never develop internal motivation or a clear, ethical stance. To achieve autonomous motivation is to execute the same course of action regardless of external forces. It is raising your hand to ask a question, even when no one else's hand is raised. This idea is not meant to discredit feats that are fueled by external motivations. However, it is important to ask if you would you have taken that same action—achieved the same feat—on your own accord. It is useful for others to suggest courses of action because that is largely how you learn how to act. Those suggestions should inform your actions, not control them. Hopefully you heed external influences and cater your own motives to include the interests of others, aiming to be naturally motivated to act for yourself as well as for others. Use external motivations to mold your methods and to establish priorities, but find internal, self-sustaining, autonomous motivation for your actions.

56. Before taking action in any situation, ensure that your motivations are in accordance with your own nature. Identify the root of your motivations for a given action, and if they are autonomous—devoid of external influences—take action with confidence. There are three steps in any given reaction: stimuli, consideration, and action. The most important step—the most relevant to your character—is consideration.

After being presented with stimuli and an influx of involuntary emotion, consider how you should respond before doing so. Focus on what you can control: the moment at hand and your actions in the present. Do not forsake the period of consideration by allowing involuntary emotional responses to drive your actions. Consider the effect that your actions could have and determine the quality of your motivation. If it seems that a given action is autonomously motivated and that it would bring about positive consequences, then you should act. Bettering the future should be the foundational motivation for your actions, so refrain from actions that you deem to have enduring, negative future consequences.

Consideration, this second component of reaction, is the interim between what you see and what you do. The more you practice and engage with your period consideration, the faster, more certain, and more powerful it will become. If you refine consideration and constantly employ it, then morally-sound, impactful actions will become more automatic, requiring only brief consideration. Use the consideration period to understand how you wish to react and allow it to drive your actions. Improve your consideration process to increase the autonomy of your actions.

52. Be sound and thorough in your thoughts so that the words and actions to follow are congruent. Actions do speak louder than words, but they speak new volumes when you act on your word. In commitments of any magnitude (lunch plans, employment, relationships, etc.), you should strive for your word to be synonymous with truth. The only way to ensure the congruence of your words and actions is to manifest your words in action. To yourself and to others, stay true to your word. That is the purest form of accountability. If your word is binding and you make a commitment, then you immediately incur responsibility—a responsibility to adhere to your word with your actions.

It may be intimidating to accept the responsibility of your own word. Instead of shying away from that responsibility and accountability altogether, just be more careful with what you say so that you only say that which you know can be supported by your future actions. Employ careful thought and consideration; adapt your period of consideration to include the question of whether you can act on what you are going to say. If you have established that you are capable of acting on your word, then you must be motivated to do so. By practicing this in your decision-making and employing careful thought when choosing your words, you can speak with confidence, knowing that your actions and words will remain congruent.

74. Immoral actions are more often caused by the practice of irrational justification than by flawed morality. People are not

inherently malevolent; it is flaws in their rationales that breed immoral actions. Each person has some definition of right and wrong—some level of morality. When someone takes an immoral action, they fabricate a reason for why that action is acceptable, even though it contradicts their morals. Irrational justification for one's actions serves to dilute and dampen the feeling of wrongdoing.

Irrational justification is merely a habit; it is not characteristic of any individual. Habits can be broken. Handle bad habits like you would a wound and treat it before it bleeds into other aspects of your life. Irrational justification is a bad habit that compounds itself and results in actions that negatively affect the world around you. Like actions, habits are malleable; they can be gradually shaped by your decisions. You can redefine your habits over time if you take calculated action to do so. Work to merge your justifications and your morals so that you will only take action if you deem it to be moral. Your justifications should be synonymous with your morals. If you make an excuse or exception to act immorally, then you are forsaking your morality and irrationally justifying your actions.

With each action you take, make incremental progress toward merging your morality and your justifications. By doing so, you will begin to recognize immoral actions for what they are, and you will have a sense of responsibility to correct them. It is essential to the development of your character to refine your habits of justification so that they are rational. Prioritize this pursuit for yourself, and have faith that others can change their habits, too. The only rational view is that the right thing is always the right thing.

69. Assuming benevolent intentions, the only regrettable actions are those done in the absence of complete effort or as a result of oversight. Every person is initially and inherently benevolent. If an individual practices irrational justification or if they have flawed morals, they still have the capacity to be benevolent. That is true for you and for everyone that you interact with. Tap into your capacity for good and bring it out of others. If you continuously act to better yourself and the world around you, then your regrets will be few. The few regrets that you do incur will not be severe. Act benevolently, and you will alleviate guilt and regret.

You should not regret anything that you do with genuinely complete effort. Your effort and attitude are the primary factors of outcome that you can control. If you have a good attitude and put forth a genuine effort, then you should experience a high-quality outcome. If you have given full effort, regardless of what the outcome is, you should not regret your actions. You may incur regret when your actions lack complete effort because it is regretful to waste the potential for a higher-quality outcome.

Oversight directly affects your ability to exude complete effort; if you lack valuable knowledge, then you are incapable of producing an optimal outcome. There must be effort in preparation as well as in the execution of your actions, for if you give full effort to a flawed approach, you will still fall short of a desired outcome. You must strive for constant and complete effort so that you are well prepared to execute at the highest possible level.

Remember that this analysis of effort and attitude assumes good intentions. Actions with good intentions cause lesser regret. However, that sort of regret is only a subset of regret as a whole. Acting to inflict pain or misfortune on others or on yourself is a sort of regret that is much more severe and taxing on your being. You will never avoid regret altogether, but by constantly acting with good intentions, your regrets will be manageable and will not burden you with much guilt. With good intentions and high-quality effort, the outcome will inevitably be positive, to some degree. Any positive outcome is better than a negative one. Negative outcomes arise from malevolent pursuits, a lack of effort, or oversight—the main sources of severe regret. An optimal, dampened severity of regret comes from working for a more positive outcome. Only expose yourself to the more desirable subset of regrets by constantly having benevolent intentions and by giving complete effort to your pursuits.

61. You should be reliable and involved in each engagement to the point where your absence is noticed and your presence is felt. If you are to involve yourself in anything, you should give your full effort to it. The most accessible and most public metric for your character is your demonstrated dedication, discipline, and effort. People notice the caliber of your effort, and it reflects on your personality and character.

It is a poor course of action to engage in an endeavor if you have no intention of giving your full effort to it. That approach neither benefits you nor those around you. The quantity of the engagements you have truly means nothing if you do not make an impactful contribution to each. Quantity may look good on the surface, but that alone is not indicative of strong character.

The purest way to become a leader is to offer your complete effort. Genuine, self-motived effort is rare, but most people can recognize it when they see it. When people recognize your unique, complete effort, they will see you as someone who is worthy and capable of leading. To clarify, this genuine effort is not an effort to win over others or to fabricate some sort of tireless work ethic. It is effort that is driven by an interest in the endeavor at hand and in achieving progress in that pursuit.

Be reliable, never waiver from complete effort, and no one will question the quality of your contributions. As a litmus test to evaluate the quality of your own efforts, determine if your absence is noticed by others and if your presence is felt. Do your colleagues, peers, or mentors notice when you miss work, a meeting, or practice? Do they wish that you were there to offer your leadership and work ethic? If not, maybe your presence is not felt. Maybe there is a greater effort that you could make for yourself, your team, or your job. Complete effort may be difficult to constantly achieve, but still strive for it. Be honest with yourself and ask if you have more to give.

64. Your principles and character grow strong as a tree does resisting the force of the wind. Remain resolute in spite of adversity. A tree is only able to stand erect and strong because it must resist the force of wind; without it, the tree would not grow to be strong and erect. Treat your character like a growing tree that must combat resistance in order to fully mature.

Abandoning your principles in response to resistance will restrict the potential of your character. People most commonly abandon their principles and convictions to be accepted, to make their life easier, or to alleviate fear. You will better-off if you remain resolute. If your character is strong and consistent, you will be accepted, it will be easier to face problems, and you will not be afraid of opposition. Adjust and fortify your character in response to adversity, and you will be better equipped to resist the wind.

28. Do not sacrifice your beliefs or priorities in order to accomplish a short-term goal or to be more compatible with another person. Use your unique personality and unwavering character to be successful in your own pursuits. Your individuality and your character should take absolute precedence. Disregarding your principles only clouds and distorts your identity. No short-term gain or the favor of any other person is worth abandoning your principles or your individuality. No strong, lasting relationship can be built from an initial lie. Always be true to yourself and resolute so that you are comfortable showing your true self to others.

50. Refrain from attribution and accept responsibility. Integrity is commonly defined as doing the right thing even when no one is looking. The greatest take-away from that definition is that you must be self-motivated in order to act with integrity. Your character is defined by both your ethical principles and your ability to adhere to those principles (even when no one is looking).

You should want to earn everything that you accomplish in life. Do not cheat; accept accountability. You can either be held accountable for everything you do or for nothing that you do. This means that your failures could be attributed to bad luck, but it also means that your successes could be attributed to good luck and considered to be uncorrelated with your own merit and efforts. There is no luxury or utility in trying to pick and choose that for which you are responsible. Instead, hold yourself accountable for each one of your actions and their consequences. If you create excuses to dodge the negative consequences of your actions, people will not entrust you with responsibilities; they will not believe that you can accomplish anything on your own. Do not attribute any of your actions or their consequences to anyone or anything else. That way, when you achieve happiness and prosperity in life, you will know that it is solely a product of your merit, efforts, and decisions.

12. The truth trumps all; honesty is always beneficial, whether it be in the short run or in the long run. You should not lie to yourself or to others, for lies breed more lies. Lying to others leads you to doubt yourself. In doubting yourself, you will arbitrarily latch on to an identity, trying to become someone that you are not. This change and adoption of an inaccurate identity would only lead you to continue to lie to others while presenting a false façade. Never offer an inaccurate portrayal of yourself so that you do not waste energy fooling yourself and others that it is the truth. Have confidence that you can find your own way, and if you are unhappy with who you are at the moment, change it. Do not change it artificially, though. Strive to define and achieve your identity by adhering to honesty.

If you lie or make excuses to avoid every negative setback, then you will never adapt your actions. Allow yourself to see reality so that you can improve it, and reveal your reality to others so that they may help you grow. Honesty is essential to integrity, and integrity is essential to the development of your character. Do not condemn you own long-term progress merely to avoid a challenge or difficulty in the moment.

11. Learn from every failure to ensure success in the future. The positive and negative aspects of thoughts and experiences are only realized through your perception and responses. The key to channeling positivity and retaining optimism is mastering the transition from mistakes to progress—from failure to success. Analyze, adapt, and react to your experiences to ensure more positive actions in the future. This sense of responsibility to learn from your experiences should be seen as an essential part of your character.

68. Your trajectory can be altered by external forces, but the severity of their impact is under your control. If you limit the weight of negative forces and limit the time that you dwell on them, their effect will be dampened. This practice is entirely necessary if you are to retain command over your path in life. Address negative forces in the mind by acknowledging your emotions and understanding your thoughts, many of which are involuntary. You have no control over your impulsive thoughts or feelings, but you can control your responses to those stimuli. Your thoughts are the scenery out your car window, and your mind is a diverse landscape of peaks and valleys—treachery and bliss. It is a landscape that you traverse at will

as the scenery passes you by. It is fleeting and always changing, just like thoughts. As you would on a road trip, you can stop and enjoy some of the beautiful scenery—your most insightful thoughts and your most impactful experiences. Conversely, uninteresting or barren landscapes should not draw your time or attention. Acknowledge those types of thoughts and experiences as being necessary to the journey, but do not allow dismal scenery to deter you from following your path or from exploring your mind. As you journey within yourself, be confident that you will reach your destination—your desired identity and character. More importantly, ensure that you enjoy the journey, for that is the only way to arrive at a desirable destination.

67. What hinders you? Ask this question of yourself when you are discouraged, and be honest. The most likely case is that any hindrance you identify is just an excuse. The power that you have to enact change is forever uninhibited. It is a power granted to the living; it is free will. You not only have free will to act, but free will to respond. You have the ability to overcome obstacles and to be unfazed by opposition. Why spend time conjuring up reasons as to why you have not or cannot reach your goals? What hinders you? What restricts you from acting how you wish or from being positive, tolerant, optimistic, driven, engaging, and empathetic? You can do it all. There is someone out there whose struggles are much more severe than your own. Maybe you can find motivation in that. Are they hindered by their obstacles, or do they strive to surmount them? Constantly remind yourself of your own abilities and recognize

excuses for what they are. You must not irrationally justify your failures or faults because then you will not learn from them. Acknowledge your mistakes and make progress in response to them. These responses will translate to incremental progress that helps shape your character as a whole. Develop and fortify your character by wielding your morals, principles, and convictions to combat oppositions to individuality.

INTERACTIONS: INCREMENTING YOUR IMPACT

1. *Always allow for the benefit of the doubt.*

The explanation or reasoning behind people's actions and opinions is often quite different than what you would assume. It is unjust to assume the causes of one's behavior or to claim to understand someone without putting forth any effort to do so. Know that everyone has their own struggles, challenges, and battles. Be conscious of that fact when making judgements or demands. This is not to say that you should release others from accountability or grant undeserved forgiveness. However, you should allow for the possibility that there is a valid rationale for something that seems irrational to you; give people the opportunity correct or explain what may seem to be a flawed course of action. Allowing for this explanation does not require that you forsake consequence and accountability. If someone makes no effort to right their wrongs, then you have no obligation to absolve them of their actions.

Be aware of the distinction between excuses and rational justifications. A single, isolated action or decision could be a reflection an individual's character, but you should not assume that it is. From one interaction with someone, you cannot understand them, and you cannot assume that the nature of that one interaction defines the whole personality of that person. You should allow for the benefit of the doubt to grant yourself the chance to dutifully engage with others—to allow yourself to withhold judgement. Deter yourself from quick judgements, and refrain from condemning individuals based on isolated instances. Judgements, by definition, are conclusions, not speculations. What you learn about others should come from your own, genuine inquisition and never from unwarranted assumptions. Make an effort to understand the nature and motives of others.

This "rule of engagement" directly relates to the Golden Rule, for everyone wants to be understood. Therefore, if you are going to treat others how they want to be treated, in accordance with the Golden Rule, then you must make an effort to understand them. You cannot begin to understand others if your perception is burdened and clouded by premature, misplaced assumptions. You must allow for the benefit of the doubt if you are to dutifully interact with others.

44. Address it. Empty space is never left empty; it fills with a narrative that is constructed based on assumptions. If something is

left unaddressed, it will not just dissipate. Instead, it will morph into something inaccurate that is predicated on others' uninformed perceptions. Do not find relief in successfully avoiding difficult conversations. Realize that what you do not address is just being addressed internally and independently by those involved. That independent thought, coupled with incomplete context, is always a worse alternative than just directly addressing the situation—having the conversation. Addressing a situation could be as simple as acknowledging a disagreement and accepting it. However, with no conversation or conclusion, people will wrestle with an idea in their mind and explore all of its possible implications. Since the issue was left to others to address independently, their perception of the event may be something completely inaccurate. Regardless of its accuracy, that perception is their reality. In the interest of efficiency and simplicity, you must collaborate with others in the pursuit of an understanding. Do not be deterred by the temporary discomfort that tough conversations bring about; the positive consequences of addressing it far outweigh your initial apprehensions about doing so.

3. Gather as much information as possible before passing judgment in any situation. There is no reason to be misinformed other than a lack of effort. In the absence of complete effort, you will have regret. The amount of information you could gather would be infinite if you were given an eternity to do so. Therefore, the quantity of information that you can gather is dependent on the time that you allocate to doing so. There should be no shortness of effort when informing your decisions and opinions. However, do not deliberate

to excess; the process of gathering information should not lead you to inaction or indecision. If your analysis of a situation causes you to forego a conclusion altogether, then your deliberation is excessive and inefficient. Learn as much as possible before the time comes to make a decision, but make sure that you still make a decision. Only pass judgment once you have achieved a significant understanding of the situation at hand. Formulate your opinion by acquiring new knowledge, and do not be dissuaded from manifesting your opinion in the form of a decision or conclusion.

73. The most suspicious, accusatory individuals are those who have either been a victim or a culprit. If you think to check for gum under your seat, you have probably either touched gum under a seat before or have been the one to put it there. Someone who is overly-cautious, anxious, accusatory, or suspicious usually has a reason to be. Maybe they were a victim of some sort and are now more cautious to avoid a similar experience. Maybe they victimized others and want to make sure not to be a victim themselves. This applies to incidents of any magnitude.

You should recognize the events that have influenced your own suspicions of others and determine if they are rational and warranted. Make a similar effort when working to understand others; if they are suspicious and surprisingly accusatory for no clear reason, then do not assume that they are personally attacking you or questioning your integrity. In the interest of allowing for the benefit of the doubt, you should assume that others are suspicious for reasons that are unrelated to you and your actions. You cannot control others' reactions. It is much easier to understand your own emotional responses, and that is what you must do if you are to control them. Within yourself, you should strive to find balance in regard to your own worries and suspicious; refrain from naiveté but also from unnecessary worries.

17. Accelerate to escape someone's blind spot. Do not slow down and fall back into their rear-view mirror. Seize opportunities, take control, and make yourself known. Do not allow others to determine your position. You should never feel comfortable in someone's blind spot. On the road, it is the most dangerous place to be, and it is in life, too. If you are riding next to someone, unnoticed, what are you going to do if they decide to change lanes? Will you honk, accelerate, brake? You would not have to respond to their actions at all if you had driven into their line of sight. If you seek comfort by moving through life unbeknownst to others, you will constantly be responding to their actions rather than acting on your own ambitions. Anonymity is dangerous, and it is not something you should long for; it relieves you of accountability but also of recognition. Your intentions and pursuits should celebrated, not shrouded and concealed. Do not hide in the shadows of others' ideas. Make yourself known and make your purpose clear. You will earn respect, gain confidence, and be more able to focus on your own journey.

21. Outward expressions of passion and dedication result in respect and admiration from others. If you are truly passionate, then you have found something that is worth pursuing. Be dedicated so

that you have the necessary discipline to consistently give time and effort to the pursuit of your passions. Everyone longs to have clarity of passion and to be sure of their priorities. What is there that is not appealing about knowing what you want to do and being fully dedicated to doing it? If it is desirable to know your passions and to follow them, then why should you ever be ashamed of doing so? You may be able conceal your passions from others, but you will still be aware of them; you cannot fool yourself. Be open with your passions so that you can more easily pursue and fulfill them. It is exhausting and taxing to conceal your identity; it takes energy to put up a front. Refrain from concealing your passions from others, as it leeches time and energy from the pursuits that are meaningful to you.

Shamelessly cling to your passions, for they will bring you happiness and help lead you to purpose. If you are worried about disgrace or shame upon revealing your passions, know that others admire passion. It is undeniably admirable to have found passion and to be disciplined enough to pursue it. People will respect and admire you for being passionate, even if they do not make it known to you. Pursue your passions with no reservations, and remain dedicated to them upon the completion of your goals and beyond.

24. Lead people; never demean people. The most effective type of leadership is that founded on mutual respect and mutually-held accountability. Earn respect by setting a virtuous example, and then encourage others to follow. You can only solicit effort from others once you have proven your own effort, capabilities, and commitment. Give complete effort and strive to adhere to lofty, self-

enforced expectations. Only then can you establish mutual respect amongst a group and begin to hold each other accountable to the same set of expectations.

Assuming a leadership role is not taking a place above others; it is taking a place in front of others. As a leader, you are not better than anyone, you are just more visible. There is a level of vulnerability that you must accept with increased visibility. Leaders are more susceptible to scrutiny and are usually unable to escape accountability. That is why not everyone seeks to lead; leadership implies added responsibility and the sacrifice of anonymity.

A true leader is respected for their efforts and followed because they reciprocate that respect. Degrading actions and words are the enemy of mutual respect. Refrain entirely from elevating yourself above someone else. Always be alongside others. If you are willing to be vulnerable and to accept additional responsibility, then step in front of others to lead.

58. Limit auxiliary interactions by exchanging pleasantries, making personal inquiries, and forming intimate connections. Interactions are what drive the human experience, so produce as many enriching interactions as you can. Simultaneously, try to reduce the frequency of impersonal, auxiliary interactions. Make interactions impactful even if that impact is just making someone smile or making their job easier. Auxiliary interactions often arise due to a lack of desire to engage with others. It is easy to allow people to enter your life briefly as a cog to turn one wheel and then let them leave, but no one else exists to serve your pursuits. Everyone is pursuing a purpose

of their own, and that is how it should be. That is how you should want it to be. Recognize that everyone has their own story and that they view themselves as the protagonist in that story. Their narrative should intrigue you, and maybe they will be intrigued by yours in return. You should give your interest and attention without expecting it to be reciprocated. If you are genuinely interested in others' pursuits, they will naturally want you to succeed in yours. Be the first to reach out and bring people together; bring people toward you.

Take the following to be general rules for interaction: (1) exchange in pleasantries with those you see in passing, (2) make personal inquiries with people that you see on a regular basis (daily, weekly, annually, etc.), and, (3) form intimate connections with those whose stories you find the most intriguing and who best reciprocate that interest.

First, what you may see to be an auxiliary interaction, such as one you would have with a cashier or barista, make it meaningful by offering pleasantries and wishing them well. Ask for people's names and use them. It is a simple way to acknowledge individuality, begin a conversation of their narrative, and express your interest in their perspective. Second, if you know that you will see someone on a routine basis, make personal inquiries. These could be as simple as questions about their past, their current ambitions, or just their opinion. Lastly, form intimate connections with those who you respect and admire and who reciprocate those sentiments.

You cannot make personal inquiries with a stranger, and you cannot meet a stranger without first exchanging pleasantries.

Therefore, no intimate connection can be formed between two people without preliminary personal inquiries and a genuine interest from both parties in the answers to those questions. These tiers of interaction are necessary to form relationships. With each new person, you must move through the tiers in sequence. Intimate connections cannot be achieved without personal inquiry, and personal inquiry cannot precede the exchange of pleasantries. Consistently engage with different people in all three tiers of interaction. It will increase your exposure to others' ideas and experiences and allow you to achieve intellectual intimacy in your relationships by increasing the quality of your interactions.

In the pursuit of intimate connections (as with anything else), practice makes perfect and preparation yields confidence. However, frequent interactions mean nothing if they are not substantive. Meaningful and enriching interactions will propel relationships, bringing them closer to intellectual intimacy. It is the density of interaction—the product of quality and quantity—that determines the depth of a relationship, not the sheer quantity of interaction. If you practice having meaningful, impactful interactions, then you will be prepared to succeed in the relationships that matter most to you. Increase the quality of your interactions by mastering each tier, and genuinely invest in others' passions and pursuits. Your relationships will have more depth, they will come easier, and your life will be enriched as a result.

62. Objects at rest tend to stay at rest unless acted upon by an external force, and conversation is such an object. Exert a force to

accelerate that object and put conversation in motion, for objects in motion tend to stay in motion. The natural state of conversation is stagnation; there must be work done if conversation is to be initiated. Do not be discouraged by the effort that takes to start a conversation; the benefits of conversation far outweigh any negative prerequisites for it. If conversation stays in motion, it increases the potential for enrichment, growth, and discovery. There is only so much analysis and growth that one can achieve with only the contents of their own mind. Ideas, opinions, and experiences are idle and benign in the absence of conversation. An individual's experiences and ideas serve no purpose to the world if they are not shared. Share your own experience and learn from others'. People want to tell their story, so be someone who expresses a genuine interest in hearing it. That is the easiest and best way to propagate conversation: express an interest in others' experiences, and be willing to discuss your own.

 89. Perpetuate and encourage the thoughts and actions that you wish to see in the world. There is no encouragement that is not worth your time to give. You must also recognize those with whom you share ideals, principles, priorities, or pursuits. It is your duty to praise others' efforts, especially if they are in pursuit of something you are passionate about or that you hold sacred. Express your support of those sorts of thoughts and actions to help further them in the world at large. Do not let your own pursuits blind you to the similar efforts of others. Through support and encouragement, you

can reach beyond just your own abilities to better the world by promoting what you want to see in it.

You should always wish others success, but there is a necessary distinction to be made between wishing someone success and actively helping them succeed. If you do not wish ill on others, then you, in turn, wish them success. That is a default, passive form of support that should always be given and received. However, for people whose thoughts and actions prompt you to think, "I wish I saw more of that in the world," you should actively help them succeed. To help someone succeed instead of just wishing them success, you must understand their pursuits and work to further them. That understanding stems from recognition and encouragement.

Define your passions and pursue purpose while encouraging and supporting others along the way. Encouragement is so powerful, and supportive interactions are essential if you are to maximize your positive impact on the world.

53. You must truly know yourself in order to dutifully interact with others. Your capacity for empathy is dependent on the level of understanding that you have of yourself, and empathy is integral to the quality and impact of your interactions. Prioritize self-discovery. Apply what you learn within the context of your own experience, beliefs, and actions so that you may gain knowledge of yourself from the world. Achieve surety of thought so that you may later have a similar surety, certainty, and confidence in your actions. Even if your thoughts are aligned with your beliefs, you may still be unsure of how

to act. If your beliefs are not consistent, then acting on them is equally unsteady and brings about uncertainty. Become more certain of your beliefs before thinking and acting on them. This self-understanding must come before you can understand others and raise your level of empathy. Empathy is entirely necessary to increment the quality of your interactions and relationships, so strive to be highly empathetic. Know that empathy can only increase after elevating your personal certainty and self-understanding. Your impact is manifested through interactions. Establish your thoughts and beliefs so that, by acting on them, you produce positive, enriching interactions that better the lives of those around you.

87. Failing due to fear is destructive, but trying and failing is constructive. There are two distinct types of failure: (1) trying and failing, and (2) failing due to inaction or a lack of effort. The former is the kind of failure that your coach is not angry about even after a loss; the latter failure is the kind that your coach preaches about for an hour after the game, even if you won. Trying and failing is considered a mistake, and you can learn from mistakes. Not trying at all, due to a fear of failing, is not a mistake but a conscious decision to forsake potential success. A fear of failure breeds inaction, which should be feared more than any consequence of action. It is irrational to fear failure, but it is rational to fear inaction; it is a threat to the potential for change. Inaction—not trying—is a sort of finality: the death of potential.

Inaction, stagnation and immobilization are the greatest enemies of progress, so never be paralyzed by a fear of failure.

Failure is progress; it is just not the ideal form of progress. There can be no innovation without a prototype. There can be no language without first uttering gibberish. There can be no maps without initial exploration. You will never regret your mistakes more than you regret missing out on what you chose not to do. Think of the inventors that feared their idea would be rejected, the linguists that feared they would be misunderstood, or the explorers that feared finding nothing along the way. Did they still try? Many of them probably did not, and the world will never know what could have come from their attempt. Those who did make an attempt, though, are the ones who gave themselves the chance to succeed. Do not convince yourself that you will fail without even trying. It may seem like you are avoiding failure by not trying, but that, itself, is the worst sort of failure. By not trying, you eliminate the possibility for success.

If you allow a problem or challenge to restrict you from taking action, then you may never find a solution. It is possible that a solution can only be reached by learning from the mistakes of your attempts; your current level of knowledge may not be enough for you to achieve success. You may need new knowledge that can only be obtained by learning from trial and error. Acknowledge failure as a possible route to success, and allow yourself to learn from your attempts.

Consider again the two aforementioned ideas: (1) do not fear failure, and (2) acknowledge the new knowledge and progress that can result from your attempts. Whatever your goal, the ideal way to reach it would be by way of constant, sustained success. That may not be a plausible route; there may have to be failures along the way. If you only acknowledge one possible route to your goal, that alone may prevent you from reaching it.

Make progress toward your goals by making attempts, not by waiting for success to be a guarantee. Refer to this specific state of self-imposed inaction as "progressive immobilization:" to forgo progress now in order to preserve your plans for future success. It is irrational to allow grand plans for the future to restrict you from acting in the present just because you know that you cannot achieve those plans right away. Continued progress is necessary to achieve future success; new levels of success cannot be achieved without prior progress.

That is progressive immobilization. It would be like if you were to allow yourself to be homeless because you have plans to own a mansion one day. You would settle for nothing less than a mansion if you were to buy a house, so you do not buy a house at all. Failure in your mind is not owning a mansion, so you never buy another house because that would be admitting failure. This is an extreme example, but it illustrates a point. With any pursuit, you should fear giving up more than you fear failing. Just because you do not yet have the means to meet your ultimate goal does not mean that you should halt progress toward it altogether. Find what you can do at the moment and do it. Make an attempt. Maybe you will make a breakthrough. The worst thing you can do is to not try. Fear that instead of fearing failure.

59. Guilt is the most invasive and pervasive sentiment. It tethers the mind to the past through the recollection of regretful actions. To be unrestrained by guilt, address your regrets and make penance. Guilt is caused by the recollection of regrets. By definition, regrets are undesirable and seem to be natural sources of guilt, but guilt can be avoided even if you have regrets. There are, however, many flawed ways that people avoid feeling guilty and avoid facing their regrets. Obviously, the best way to avoid guilt is to never commit regretful acts, but that is an unrealistic expectation for yourself and for others. You can, however, make penance for the actions that you regret. Many people will refuse to make penance for their actions because they worry that acknowledging a mistake will cause them to incur more guilt. That mindset is flawed. You will make mistakes, as everyone does, so acknowledge them; use them productively.

Among the worst ways to respond to a mistake is to lessen it in your mind by convincing yourself that the impact of it was not as severe as it seemed. Just acknowledge mistakes for what they are. Otherwise, you will not be able to fully address them or make penance. One possible extension of unaddressed regret is that you remove people from your life due to an inability to reconcile your own actions. You should never reach that point. Do not make your own guilt an external issue; deal with it yourself and do not project blame for it onto others. Your regrets are your problem and no one else's. Address them so that you can preserve and improve your interactions and relationships. You can eliminate regrets, but only by identifying them and then working to make penance. That is the only valid way to alleviate guilt.

You should want to avoid guilt, largely because it impedes your progress and abilities by anchoring your thoughts to past actions and events. It leaches away at the time that you have in the present, which has a negative impact on your future.

In the process of avoiding regretful actions, do not lower your expectations or avoid interactions out of a fear of incurring guilt. Yes, if you expect less of yourself, maybe you will fail less (relative to those low expectations) and maybe feel less guilty. However, if your potential for failure and regret is lowered, then the same happens for your potential for success and pride.
Inform your actions with consistently high expectations. Your goal should be to automatically complete actions that others would struggle to commit to out of a fear of regret. Know how you wish to act, always expecting yourself to act as such. If you constantly act in the interest of yourself and others, then you will limit regretful actions and alleviate guilt. Instead of your regrets consisting of the times that you did not act because of fear, the worst of your regrets will be the times that you did not give your full effort. You will start to regret mistakes rather than missed opportunities. As a result, the regrets you do have will be less of a burden, and it will be easier to make penance for them; it will be easier to alleviate guilt. Address regret head-on so that you can correct your behavior, staving off future regretful actions. Empower yourself with ownership of and timely responses to regret so that you may be unimpeded by guilt.

99. Employ logos and pathos to solidify your ethos, or credibility. Do not assume that your credibility is recognized or accepted; prove it by logically explaining your methods and clearly illustrating your passions. You should never find yourself explaining to someone that you are credible. They should be telling you that they believe you are credible, based on their understanding of your experiences and personality. Others will not believe that you are credible based on your word because you have not yet proven the validity or merit of your word. It is essential to understand that. Why would someone trust you if they are unsure of your credibility? Why would saying that you are credible make you any more so? People will always doubt your credibility if all you do is make a claim to it. You must establish genuine credibility through mutual trust and respect with others. The responsibility that others give to you is dependent on your perceived level of credibility, and you should want to be trusted with added responsibility. Therefore, strive to establish genuine credibility.

Citing your status or previous experience as a reason to be respected or trusted is an indication of an inflated ego. Your opinion of yourself should matter to you, but it matters much less to everyone else. You should aim to earn respect by appealing to others' logic and emotions. Allow others to grant you respect and credibility instead of trying to pry it out of them or acting as though you deserve it outright.

The most common way to logically sway someone into giving you responsibility is to cite your experience. While that may be a valid reason for you to be given responsibility and credibility, the person who is evaluating you did not share those experiences with you. Instead of merely citing the quantity of your experience, you should work to illustrate the impact of your actions in your previous engagements and endeavors. Here, logos and pathos converge. The quantity of your experience is certainly relevant, so use logos to communicate it. Combine that fact with pathos by explaining your impact on others and how your experiences have impacted you. It is logical to grant merit to someone with many years of experience in a given field, but their level of deserved merit is not fully communicated without an explanation of how well they have applied their knowledge and experience.

You should find yourself proving your worth rather than claiming to be worthy. Similarly, and simultaneously, it is your duty to determine if others are worthy, not accepting their claims of worth outright. You should only grant someone trust once they have proven their worth by appealing to your logic and emotions. Look for people that couple a sound rationale with emotional intelligence. Identifying logos and pathos in others will bolster your own ability to employ those skills. Develop your skills of logos and pathos so that you increase the rate at which you detect empty claims of credibility.

The pillars of logos, pathos, and ethos are often seen as separate entities that independently deliver information. In fact, they work in tandem and quite often blend together. A better way to view them is as follows: Ethos is the house that you build for yourself where logos acts as bricks and pathos as mortar. You live within your ego, and much of it (the exterior of your house) is exposed to the rest of the world. With bricks and mortar, you are given the ability to determine the dimensions of your ego and the appearance of it to others. Bricks can be stacked without mortar, but that sacrifices the stability and integrity of your house. Without any ties to emotion, logic presents a weak façade and gives your credibility no chance at longevity. Mortar, spread between just two bricks, is inconsequential to the fortitude of your house as a whole. Without logic to cling to, emotion is useless to the construction and cohesion of your credibility.

You must combine logos and pathos to construct your ethos. Your house should be built tall with bricks and fortified with mortar. Sound logic can only come from the pursuit of knowledge, and strong pathos can only come from elevated empathy. Pursue both knowledge and empathy so that you know your own worth and have the necessary tools to communicate credibility and identify it in others.

81. The time you have to impact the world is finite, but the ramifications of your actions are infinite. Take advantage of the time you have now to learn about yourself, determine how you wish to impact the world, and do so by dutifully interacting with others. Do not sink into stagnation; further your pursuits as well as others' in the hopes of helping humanity succeed. Interactions are powerful because they increment experiences in life while simultaneously allowing you to impart your influence on others. No interaction should be taken for granted, and each should be treated with the

utmost respect and importance. You truly do not know the impact that a given interaction can generate. The quantity of your interactions is limited by your lifespan, but the quality of them and the impact that you impart are unbounded by time and are solely dependent on your efforts. The ramifications of your actions are infinite, so dutifully interact with others so that your infinite impact is positive.

RELATIONSHIPS:
VEHICLES FOR ENJOYMENT AND FULFILLMENT

71. Know yourself well so that you are able to detect incongruences in your actions, as to not damage your relationships with others.

The relationship that you have with yourself is more important than any other. In regard to that relationship, you should evaluate yourself and be able to correct any transgressions against what you have established as your own nature. After realizing a negative change in the nature of your actions—in your general conduct—engage in self-reflection. Identify and address what is distracting you from adhering to your nature. Just because you know how you want to act does not mean that you are always successful in doing so; merely establishing guidelines is not the same as consistently following them. Frequently evaluate your actions and their effect on others to determine how well you are adhering to your nature.

By constantly and honestly evaluating whether you are doing the right thing, you will never be unsure of whether you are doing the right thing. To have certainty in the evaluation of your actions, you must know how you wish to act, and you must be honest with yourself when classifying the nature of your actions. Recognize right and wrong for what it is and determine whether your actions meet your expectations. Uncertainty in yourself breeds discomfort, a lack of direction, and a lack of confidence. If you do something that is contrary to your nature, you should be able to evaluate it as such, with complete certainty. Similarly, you must acknowledge the frequency at which you *do* act in accordance with your nature. That positive recognition improves the relationship you have with yourself and increases self-confidence.

The relationship that you have within is the most important because it informs your thoughts and actions, which determine how well you will be able to form connections with others. If you can be sure of anything in any relationship, it should be surety in regard to yourself and your own actions.

84. Widen the breadth of your experience so that you may hone the accuracy of your empathy. There are generally three forms of emotional response: apathy, sympathy, and empathy. If you are to make any attempt at being caring and compassionate toward others, you must refrain from apathy; it is contrary to the formation of any relationship and to the provision of emotional support. Assuming

that you hope to be compassionate, you should employ sympathy and empathy in your interactions and relationships. Yes, it is good and noble to be sympathetic to others' situations, but if you can transmute sympathy into empathy, the connections that you forge and the support you provide will be even stronger.

The distinction between sympathy and empathy is that if you are sympathetic, you have no shared experience to reference or to offer. You can only empathize with someone if you have a personal understanding of their experience. The development of any relationship is fundamentally dependent on your ability to employ empathy. Your capacity for empathy is proportional to your understanding of others' experiences. If you wish to elevate your ability for empathy, then you must widen the breadth of your experience. Prioritize the development of empathy because the success of your relationships is dependent on it.

Empathy is propagated by the diversity of your experience, and the quality of your relationships is dependent on your ability to empathize. Therefore, it is desirable and beneficial to expand your realm of personal experience so that you may relate to a higher quantity of people. Experience can be derived from nearly everything: education, interactions, travel, performance, competition, etc. Reach into every corner of the realm of human experience to enrich yourself and elevate your empathy.

7. Never be afraid to engage with people. You never know what a new relationship or a single interaction could bring. There are so many connections, similarities, and common experiences that you

share with others. Explore how you align with others as well as how you contradict. By seeking out interpersonal interactions, you will learn to be more engaging, to capture attention, and to communicate your own ideas. If you do struggle to initiate interaction, start with trying to find something in common. You will find that social connections are the easiest commonalities to uncover, so try to identify a mutual friend. In this pursuit, there will usually be much less than six degrees of separation. Ask a question as simple as, "where are you from?" It opens the door for conversation and greatly increases the chances of creating connections. Bridge the gap between stranger and acquaintance, between acquaintance and friend, and between friend and companion. Constantly initiate interactions. The practice of doing so will strengthen your social abilities, improve your oratory skills, and enrich your intellect.

Consider the fact that the positive potential of an interaction far outweighs the negative possibilities of it. Engaging with others could deepen your relationships or create new ones. It could help you solve a problem or reveal one that you had never considered. Look for intellectual growth through interaction, and improve your capacity for empathy by engaging with others.

34. Places are the stuff of the most vivid memories. Experience places in an intimate way, and use those places to form more intimate relationships with the people that you share them with. Time may seem to accelerate when you are trying new things and slow down when you are doing routine, mundane acts. For new experiences, memories are deeper and more vivid; memories of

routine actions are cloudy and diluted in comparison. There is naturally more energy dedicated to the intake of new information than there is to the intake of information that is predictable or familiar.

Travelling is the best, most common, and most accessible way to have new experiences and create new memories. New places require you to take in all sorts of unfamiliar and unpredictable information. As a result, the memories you have of places are often the most vivid sorts of memories. Look for new experiences everywhere you go; explore your hometown, expose yourself to culture, and find views that only few have looked upon.

Enhance your experiences in new places by the way in which you engage with the people around you. Connect with others in new places so that you may strengthen your personal relationships by sharing in the wonder of exploration. New experiences are invaluable, and impactful memories urge you to experience and explore more. Do not be satisfied to tread along the surface; you should dive deep into new places because there are even more novel experiences that lie there. Engage with places in such a way that the experience you have is meaningful to the people you share it with.

4. Keep objects that remind you of the past and collections that continue into the future. A healthy relationship with the past is one that simply reminds you of what brought you to the present. It is ideally a relationship that is rooted in gratitude and pride. A practical tool that is useful in fostering such a relationship is collections. Regardless of how proud you are of your past or how happy you are

in the present, there are moments that influenced your outlook, that enriched your mind, or that brought you joy. Maintaining collections is a simple way to take the time to acknowledge the impact that an experience had on you. Then, when you refer to the past, your evaluation is not just a binary classification of whether your past is good or bad. Instead, you have identified enriching experiences as well as those that were less desirable. Continually collect objects that remind you of the past so that you realize the nature and utility of enriching experiences.

8. Ask often and wonder freely. Everyone shares in uncertainty, and others likely have the same questions that you do. A common concern could lead to an interaction, a relationship, or a solution. The worst end for any unanswered question is for it to wither away inside your mind, never to be pursued or posed to anyone else. Having nearly no knowledge of a topic should not discourage you from pursuing it. Instead, wonder and uncertainty should be catalysts for the acquisition of knowledge. Asking questions does not (or should not) diminish anyone's perception of your intelligence. If your questions are purposeful and thoughtful, they will actually enhance others' perception of your intelligence. If you are at all interested in learning, then you should not be averse to inquisition. Many people are too quick to assume that they understand. Frequently, people will decide not to ask a clarifying question out of a fear of looking unintelligent. Instead, they choose to look disinterested in the topic at hand. You should strive to ask those clarifying questions if they are needed. It does not hurt to ask.

Clarify in order to move forward with a clearer understanding. Then, you can continue to explore new, unknown territory and not shy away from it by acting artificially disinterested.

The unique power of questioning is that it is a self-fueling endeavor; the more questions you ask, the more questions you will have. Find comfort in that. It only takes consideration and wonder to produce more questions and further your understanding. You acquire new knowledge through questioning. If questioning propels itself, then so does the pursuit of knowledge. There is no limit to intellectual growth because there is no limit to questioning or to knowledge itself. Inquisition is your primary tool in the pursuit of knowledge. Give life to the questions you have by asking without hesitation or reservation. You will be surprised by how many others have similar lines of thought or similar desires for answers and solutions. By publicly posing a question, you can more expediently reach a solution and maybe form a personal connection while doing so. Unite with others to achieve intellectual growth. People will appreciate your shameless questioning; it will invigorate their intellect and often spark a special thought, experience, or breakthrough. When you ask a question, whether the result is a new discovered truth or merely a funny realization, it is better than anything that would come from forsaking that question and allowing it to fade to the back of your mind.

20. Teach how to think, not what to think. Consider the idea of thought-provoking vs. thought-demanding. Would you be more inclined to think and learn if you were ordered or encouraged to do

so? The distinction between teaching how to think and teaching what to think lies in your relationship with inquisition. If one is bombarded with questions and solicited only for solutions, there is little opportunity for them to develop thoughts and questions of their own.

If you are in the position to educate, coach, or instruct, you should introduce thoughts and questions in an effort to provide a launching point for the student to think for themselves. Teach students about the mountain and give them the tools to climb it, but do not require them to take a certain trail. Give the student credit; the more responsibility one is given to ask questions of their own, the more they will believe they are capable of learning—the more they will be drawn to further inquisition. One's ability to produce solutions to a narrow realm of questions may indicate their current level of knowledge, but it does not speak to their aptitude for acquiring new knowledge. Inquisition is essential to the pursuit of knowledge; knowing how to learn is knowing how to ask questions, not knowing how to answer them.

Rigid definitions and narrow lines of questioning are practices that further the separation between one's perception and reality. The acquisition of knowledge should serve to match one's perception to reality. Students and individuals in general should be taught to consider every facet of any given field. Limited lines of questioning restrict the bounds of an individual's imagination. To learn best, one must know that there is no limit to the questions they can ask, to the connections they can find, or to the information that they can acquire.

One way to consider the process of learning is to think of it as likening your perception to reality. The more you learn and understand, the closer your personal perception is to truth itself. This sort of learning cannot be achieved without the consideration of others' perceptions, for no one person's perception is reality. Reality is the aggregate of perception; it is the sum of all perceptions that define it. Consider alternate interpretations rather than ignorantly clinging to a single one. When an individual acknowledges the validity of others' perceptions and definitions, then they can improve their knowledge and the quality of their own perception by exploring those new ideas. As an educator, you should not force your perspective because your perspective is only part of reality. If your students are likening their perspective to yours, then they are not learning efficiently because they are only exposed to a portion of reality. Regarding your own pursuit of knowledge, do not restrict your own realm of inquisition by ignoring others' perceptions. Each individual has something new to offer. Everyone's perception is part of reality—part of truth.

To live in accordance with the Golden Rule, you must consider others' perspectives. Everyone longs to be understood, and if you are to treat others as they want to be treated, you must strive to understand their view. Failing to value someone's ideas is a failure to dutifully interact with that person. Skills such as empathy, communication, and open-minded thinking are founded in the idea of mutual understanding. A mutual understanding cannot be achieved without the realization that no single perception, not even your own, can define reality. You must value others' perceptions if you value truth.

As an educator, provide the means of exploration with no restrictions on the journey itself; teach how to think, not what to think. As a student, do not limit the scope of your exploration. Leverage inquisition and open-mindedness to incrementally liken your perception to reality.

45. Heed the voices of history; the brevity of human existence is most evident in the relevance of elder commentaries. For humans, as a species, there is so much more to collectively learn and explore. The youth and brevity of humanity is evident when you consider the content of historical commentaries. We are still facing the same general problems that humans did hundreds of years ago. When it comes to the discussion of technology or material progress, the voices of history may not be relevant. However, in regard to the human condition and human nature, not time or any amount of progress can taint the validity or relevance of someone's thoughts. Human nature is enduring, even though the nature of daily life has changed drastically. You should realize the relevance of anyone's comments on humanity itself, for they are valuable even if they are not nearly contemporary. Find comfort in the fact that parts of humanity are somewhat constant. Turn your ear to the voices of the past and recognize the validity of your current thoughts. Note the

progress that humanity has made, knowing that there is still infinite potential for new growth.

77. You should only make connections with dynamic entities because change is inevitable. It is detrimental to your personal progress to associate with static entities, for anything averse to change is contrary to nature. The past is a static entity; it is intrinsically immune to change. Therefore, you should not cling to the past or associate with it in a manner that causes your present actions to be restricted by it. Dynamic entities should be the root of your connections, not volatile, ever-changing entities but solid entities that are also flexible. These entities could be people, experiences, careers, or locations. In each relationship and connection that you create, retain and fortify own ability to be dynamic; adapt and respond to change. You automatically learn from the relationships you create, so make sure to connect with people and things that you want to learn from. If you are disposed to respond negatively to change, then do not tether yourself to the past. The past is fixed; it knows nothing of change. Therefore, the past cannot teach you how to enact or respond to change. Form relationships with dynamic people and dynamic entities. Those connections will fuel your present and future endeavors instead of restricting them.

95. Good-natured people will respect you for having independent views rather than disrespect you because your views differ. You should strive to be a good-natured person, and you should seek only to form close relationships with other good-natured people. Two integral parts of good, sound character are open-

mindedness and respect. If someone is incapable of respecting alternative or opposing viewpoints, then they are closed-minded and could very well hinder your personal progress.

Know that disagreement and respect are not mutually exclusive. In sports, for example, there are certainly opposing views, but respect is expected to still be fully present. If you do not respect your opponent, then you are a poor sport, and you could look like a fool if you end up losing. The better alternative is to respect competition itself for the value it brings and to compete with respect.

A good metric for the quality of your conduct—your sportsmanship—is whether your opponent wants to beat you or if they want to see you fail. The former is natural and encouraged in the context of competition, but the latter means that your opponent wishes ill on you because of your conduct, probably because you are disrespectful. In sports, you should respect your opponent's desire to succeed in competition. You and your opposition both share that desire, and there would be no competition at all if that were not the case. The positive potential for growth that competition brings would be lost if neither side had a desire to win. However, do not be disrespectful or act so that others want to see you fail. Mutual respect is lost when someone wants their opponent to lose instead of wanting to win, themselves. To wish failure on someone else only impedes your own potential for success. In tennis, for example, you should do not applaud your opponent's unforced errors. Praise the successes of who you root for instead of celebrating the failures of who you root against.

What is found in sports is true for all sorts of competition and for opposing perspectives; mutual respect is essential. The more one party disregards the other's viewpoint, the more the two will want the opposing view to be shattered and disproven. In that case, there is no hope for compromise or unified growth. That approach to disagreement even eliminates the possibility of fortifying of your own ideas. Maybe you would have won the argument, or at least figured out a new way to articulate your viewpoint. Without mutual respect, there can be no collaborative, intellectual progress. You should want to articulate your position better than the opposition, so use disagreement as a way to fortify and enrich your perspective. When forming relationships, find people who have respect for opposing views, for only good-natured people will act as such.

When you encounter opposition in your relationships or otherwise, be eager and willing to defend your own perspective; do not concede. At the same time, though, do not wish ill on your opponent. You must establish respect for the opposition before you can expect the same in return. Develop that trait for yourself, and find good-natured people who will reciprocate respect and open-mindedness.

55. Do not wish ill on others, for that action distracts you from your own pursuits of happiness, knowledge, and self-improvement. If you believe that others must fail for you to succeed, then you will struggle to achieve. Regardless of what you pursue, you will need people to help you along the way. That does not mean that you constantly need other people to actively work with you, but you

do not ever want people working against you. On your end, you should prioritize your pursuits without wishing ill on others, for they will wish ill on you in return.

Be sure to realize that your level of future success is partially dependent on the quality of your relationships. The easiest way to extinguish a relationship is to wish ill on that person, so refrain from doing so. It is just a waste of energy that is detrimental to your own efforts. You should be in favor of universal growth and progress, promoting everyone's success as well as your own. Prioritize your pursuits and the development of your relationships while wishing the best for everyone along the way.

70. It is not enough to know that you respect someone; they must know it too. Show respect with your actions and your words toward others. Respect is fundamental to the establishment, strength, and longevity of any relationship. Therefore, it is essential that you respect others and actively display it. If you are impressed, proud, pleasantly surprised, or grateful in response to someone's actions, then express that to them. Among the best ways to show respect is through support and consideration. To be respectful, you must first place value on others' ideas and hold their unique perspectives in high regard. That is essential, and it should be something that you do without exception.

For the people that you greatly respect and those that you support and care for, you must actively communicate your respect. Give time and consideration to their propositions, understand their aspirations, and encourage them to pursue their goals. Articulate the impact and the positive influence that they have on your life. By communicating your respect for others, more mutual respect will manifest itself in your relationships. Try to notice how your views of someone may differ from what they think your views of them are. If someone's perception is that you do not respect them but you know that you do, then you have not adequately communicated your respect. Use others' perceptions to inform how well you communicate your thoughts, feelings, and beliefs. In your relationships, if there is an incongruence between your feelings and others' perceptions of them, address it, and act to remedy that discrepancy.

25. Remind friends of their inner potential and aptitude, ensuring that they acknowledge their own greatness. The most important relationship is the one you have with yourself. Recognize that the same is true for everyone else. In your relationships, you should examine how other people view themselves and try to help improve their self-image. Your relationship with someone should contribute positively to the relationship that they have with themselves.

Be confident enough in your capacity for empathy and understanding that you frequently boost others' self-confidence. That support does not come from empty, ready-made compliments. You must gain an understanding, recognize insecurities, and then help others grow and overcome. There is no need to lie or patronize, though. These are people that you support and care for, so remind them of their potential while holding them accountable for their mistakes, too. Often, it is the case that all someone needs is some encouragement. In your closest, deepest relationships, be there to encourage genuinely and encourage often by reminding others of their infinite capacity and true greatness.

38. Never feel entitled to respect; it must be earned and achieved on an individual basis. No previous, isolated example of interpersonal success warrants automatic respect. It must be given before it is received, and in a relationship, respect must be given constantly. To believe that you are entitled to respect means forsaking the idea that respect should be mutual, and that would hinder your ability to form relationships. Do not cite other relationships to prove your character to others. You should expect to build every relationship from the ground up, and it would benefit you to become adept at doing so. If your older sibling was the best student and teacher's pet in school, that does not mean that you can strut into that same class expecting the teacher to respect you outright. Think highly of yourself, but do not expect others to share that opinion. Earn respect by being respectful.

49. Express gratitude, and do not expect it. You should have no reservations when expressing gratitude; do not make excuses for why it is not necessary to communicate your appreciation for others. Refrain from convincing yourself that the people in your life are already aware of your appreciation for them; err on the side of overcompensation when it comes to gratitude. Acknowledge the support, care, and opportunities that others provide for you so that you do not take them for granted.

If you want to ensure that you do not take something for granted, measure it by alternatives. Often, a realistic alternative is much less desirable than your current reality. Be grateful that what you are experiencing is not, instead, a worse alternative. If you deem a feasible, attainable alternative to be *more* desirable, then you should pursue it. You can be satisfied with and grateful for what you have while still wanting to grow, progress, and improve your quality of life. However, do not let that desire for growth make you lose sight of what you have now.

Grant gratitude without expectation; it will foster mutual respect as well as healthy, positive communication in your relationships. Again, consider the alternative. What if you never acknowledged what others did for you? How would you feel if you never got a "thank you," and how would you respond? You would probably start giving less to and expecting less of that person. That leads to apathy and the dissolution of a relationship. To avoid this, you need only to express gratitude. Do so, and your relationships will be stronger, healthier, and more fluid. Others will be more willing to support you with your own endeavors because they know that you appreciate their efforts. Reciprocate that appreciation and aid in others' pursuits without expecting praise for it. That is the key to emotional balance and social prosperity.

100. Be open with others; vulnerability is not synonymous with weakness. Develop the relationship that you have with yourself so that you can be confident in your identity and more willing to share yourself with others. The more you open up to others, the

more they will open up to you. You should want people to be open with you, and you should want to be approachable. If you are open and approachable, then, from your relationships, you can learn more about yourself, about others, and about life in general. To be vulnerable is to offer personal information without protection or collateral. If you concede to share on the condition that someone shares in return, then you are not truly opening up or being vulnerable.

To be willing to be vulnerable, you must be sure of yourself; no one can be vulnerable if they lack confidence. Confidence is an objectively strong and desirable trait. If vulnerability is a direct product of confidence, then it too is desirable. Let vulnerability serve as a catalyst in all of your relationships. You must build every relationship from the ground up, but if you are ready and willing to open up at the start, that process becomes expedient and enjoyable. If you are good-natured and of good character, then being exposed to others does not show weakness; it reveals your strength. Therefore, you should be voluntarily vulnerable so that you can build more relationships and connections with others while strengthening those that you have already established.

AMBITIONS:
THE PEAKS OF LIFE'S MOUNTAIN RANGE

5. Continually be aware of your interests, desires, and goals.

Ambition is the ability to convert dreams into reality, and it is the primary factor in determining how efficiently you find fulfillment, success, and satisfaction in life. However, there can be no ambition without direction; goal-setting and self-awareness are essential practices if you are to be ambitious. Knowing who you want to be and where you want to go is the biggest step in getting there.

Clearly define and articulate your goals and desires because you will begin to realize the path that you must take to reach them. Once you have identified your aspirations, the next steps will become apparent. Just decide to wholeheartedly pursue that path. Do not rely on the future to grant your wishes. You must employ ambition now to reap the benefits of success in the future. Goals and aspirations change over time, though, and they should. Pivoting and refining is inherent to the pursuit of goals itself, for you cannot see the complete path to achieving something at any point along the way. You can only see a few steps ahead, so you must incrementally adjust your course along the way. Do not blindly go down one path. Imagine a sailboat traveling from point A to point B. Is its path a straight line? It may look like it from a distant, aerial view, but in reality, the sailboat zigzags across the water. It slightly but continually adjusts its heading to ensure that it does not stray from its overall direction, orienting itself toward point B. The only way to arrive efficiently and effectively at a destination is to consider your heading along the way and adjust accordingly. Ensure that you do so in life. Constantly consider your goals so that what you are actively pursuing is congruent with what you truly hope to achieve.

65. You could rely on changing yourself in the future, or you could change right now. The only way to become who you are supposed to be in the future is to be who you want to be in the present. What reason do you have to not pursue what you deem to be desirable? Are there really insurmountable forces that prohibit you from acting how you hope to act? Take accountability now by recognizing who you are, relative to who you want to be. If you are far off from your ideal self, then you should get to work. Recognizing your position, relative to where you want to be, is what will allow you to become who you are supposed to be.

You forsake your potential by forsaking the present, which is an opportunity for growth, progress, and positive change. If you do know who you want to be, pursue it, and if you do not, take pause in the present to look inward and identify your passions. Be passionate about your most interesting interests, and follow your passions to find purpose. Act now; the future is constantly approaching, but your actions in the present determine what it brings. Be who you wish you were. Maximize your potential by capitalizing on the present to eventually become who you are meant to be.

15. Competition provides some of the most valuable experiences, as well as long-lasting life lessons. Two of the most accessible lessons to glean from competition are that (1) you should develop mutual respect with the opposition and that (2) you must not allow short-term failures to impact your long-term goals. Both of these ideas are so prevalent in competition—they are very clear to see in sports, for example. If your opponent does best you, it should not deter you from pursuing your long-term goals. Momentary discomfort, pain, failure, and loss should serve as catalysts for work and progress, not as mental inhibitors. Assign a purpose to failure instead of just letting it fester and rot into the future. Slap a new façade on the storefront of failure to later rebrand it as success. These two valuable, long-lasting, universally applicable life lessons are reason enough to promote and engage in competition. Foster mutual respect for your opponent, and do not deny the obvious benefits of competition; it is a catalyst for progress and innovation.

19. The pursuit of scientific knowledge is the pursuit of human progress. The growth and advancement of social progress is equally as important as that of technological progress; the caliber of

human relations and a depth of culture are both tightly linked to the quality of human life. However, scientific progress is more quantifiable and arguably more malleable social progress. There are clear, cause-and-effect relationships that stem from new scientific knowledge. Scientific exploration and discovery are capable of altering the structure of society itself, and those pursuits should not be stifled. The application of new knowledge should be calculated and controlled, but the acquisition of new knowledge should be forever uninhibited and considered to be a top priority on a global scale.

31. Possibly the greatest pursuit in life is that of knowledge and the application of discovered truths. To be fulfilled in life is to pursue a purpose, but what is the purpose of life? What pursuits will lead you to it? For the sake of explanation, take knowledge and happiness to be the only two possible pursuits in life. If you were to value the pursuit of happiness over the pursuit of knowledge, then you may fabricate happiness with ignorance, choosing to avoid harmful truths. In pursuing knowledge, though, you would seek to know all truths, regardless of how hard they are to accept. You can pursue happiness and knowledge simultaneously; the acquisition of knowledge does not have to involve forsaking happiness.

For you to be able to seek knowledge *and* achieve happiness, you might have to redefine what makes you happy. Are you only happy when you are comfortable? If so, then you are happy being stagnant, and it is difficult to find purpose if you never strive to grow. There is nothing wrong with choosing comfort over growth or ignorance over knowledge, but that choice does restrict you from fulfilling your potential. Discovering new truths should bring you happiness because progress should bring you happiness, and learning is objectively a form of growth and progress.

There is no end to knowledge, so there is no limit to progress that can be achieved by acquiring knowledge. It is a pursuit that facilitates continuous change and development. Contrarily, happiness is finite, and it can be defined as anything—it is subjective. The pinnacle of happiness can be achieved just by declaring that you have reached it. Knowledge is a quantifiable pursuit, and a lack of knowledge is clear, where a lack of happiness may not be. A state of objective incompletion promotes growth and development, for if something is undoubtedly incomplete, there is no logical reason to be completely satisfied with it. Why be complacent with what you know when you are aware that there is much more to learn? On the other hand, subjective incompletion introduces speculation as to whether there is a need for progress at all. If there is no desire for progress, then there is no opportunity for growth. Find happiness in the acquisition of knowledge, and do not forsake knowledge or indulge in ignorance for the sake of finding happiness.

35. Human progress is like wading through water with variable depth. The water accumulates at a constant rate, but the rate at which it drains varies. When the drain is clogged by stagnation, monotony, or conflict, the water level rises, making it harder to move forward. Conversely, when there is discovery, innovation, or revolution, the drain is cleared, and the water level lowers to a much

more manageable depth. Prioritize progress so that humanity may wade forth with ease.

With quick wits, constant consideration, and sound thought, you can sublimate stages of progress. Sublimation is the process of skipping a state of matter when transitioning from one to another. The most common example of this process is the sublimation of dry ice. When dry ice starts to heat up, or melt, it does not melt into a liquid; it sublimates by skipping the liquid stage, transitioning directly to carbon dioxide gas. Use every tool at your disposal and aim to progress at a rate similar to sublimation. That does not mean that you should desire to constantly change states, but there is no harm in efficiently achieving growth by prioritizing innovation and easing the flow of human progress.

51. Expand your own realms of comfort and knowledge so that you may know more and do more in the future and in the present. Your knowledge is dwarfed by your capacity for it. What you know now is not nearly the limit of your comprehension, nor is it an exhaustive understanding of the universe. As you learn, you discover more that there is to know. That should excite you! Continue to seek knowledge so that you become more comfortable with what you already know and that which you have already experienced. If you frequently experience discomfort and uncertainty, then you will become more comfortable with being uncomfortable. You will become less averse to venturing outward in the pursuit of knowledge and new experiences.

42. Travel so that unfamiliar places and situations become more comfortable and common. Your relationship with the unknown should be one of wonder, not one of fear. Exploration is the source of discovery. By physically exploring the world, you can learn both about the world within you as well as that which surrounds you. The more you explore, the more commonplace and comfortable it will be to do so. If you are more comfortable and confident with exploration, then you will also be more comfortable with new discoveries and the acquisition of knowledge.

76. If you did not get better at something, then you wasted a day. This rule should be applied with the goal of accurately and continually identifying progress. Realize that, in any given day, you can make strides in any aspect of life. If you fail to progress in one respect, ensure that it does not affect your engagement with the rest of your life. The simplest division of the components of daily life is to classify each experience as either personal or professional. If you are unsatisfied with the progress that you made in your professional life one day, do not allow that to weaken your personal relationships and interactions, too. The same is true for any pursuit, passion, hobby, or goal; if you fail to improve in one area, progress in another, and you will never waste a day. This practice will improve your disposition and your level of optimism. If you can hedge your failures with other successes, you will net positive progress. That is to say that you will fall softer on bad days and control how high you fly on good ones. Strive for this sort of control over your emotions and

reactions because it will bring you confidence, hope, and optimism. You will be better equipped to pursue future endeavors.

88. There is duality in everything. Understand extremes so that you can achieve balance. Are you an entertainer, an appeaser, or a leader? Really, you should never be only one. Consider each at their extremes. If you live to entertain others, you may often compromise your self-image for the sake of others' enjoyment. To live appeasing others is to constantly forsake your own pursuits and opinions to avoid confrontation. Finally, if you identify as a leader and only as a leader, then you will have no one that is willing to follow you. These extremes are detrimental to your personal progress and individuality, so do not identify as just one of them.

Arguably the most important of the aforementioned extremes is the leader. In the case of leadership, it is your character and skills as a whole that classify you as a leader, not the fact that you claim to be one. People will recognize disparities between the skills that you claim to have and those that you actually possess. To expect to lead in every endeavor is to be ignorant of the knowledge that you lack, blinding you from opportunities to learn from others. You must find balance when formulating your identity and pursuing your aspirations.

Entertain others with confidence and positivity. Aim to please, but do not appease. Lead only when you feel a genuine calling to do so. Balance is forged in compromise; you must yield ground in order to gain more in the long run. You should not cling to any one characteristic as your identity; blend traits and allow each to shine.

Temper dominant characteristics to make room for others, but do not concede any aspect of you character in its entirety. Instead, strip the negative parts from each characteristic and retain the positives: from a short temper, retain passion; from indecision, prudence; from naivety, imagination. Transform undesirable traits by dissolving the negative parts of them, and sift through each trait to uncover hidden value. The purely positive, desirable traits that remain are tapered down and less cumbersome. It vacates space in your identity, freeing you to grow and diversify the characteristics that define you.

Sift through the generic identities of the entertainer, the appeaser, and the leader to uncover and utilize the value in each of them. Yes, it is easier to subscribe to a ready-made identity and to live that out as expected by others, but do not relinquish individuality merely to satisfy your desire to be understood. Analyze your own nature and characteristics. The better you know yourself, the easier it will be to show others who you are—fully and truly. Only then can you be understood as you want to be.

78. Busyness is healthy and constructive; it helps develop the important skill of time management. While it may seem undesirable to be busy, in fact, busyness is essential to maximizing productivity. Busyness will cause you to compromise some free time, but free time is often wasted anyway. What part of inactivity is so desirable? If you are striving to find purpose, then each of your actions should be meaningful and in the service of that pursuit. Even relaxation should be efficient and not excessive. Instead of dreading the free time that you lose on account of busyness, revel in the productivity that it

brings. If you are busy, time will seem to move slower, for you are always moving relative to time. If you are stagnant and immobile, then time will pass you by much faster than if you are progressing—moving forward alongside time. If you shift from immobility to busyness, then you are more efficiently and more effectively managing your time because any level of busyness is better than lingering in limbo. Time management is among the most important skills in life because it is applicable to each day and to any endeavor. To effectively manage your time, you must be able to plan, prioritize, and execute. If being busy requires you to practice these skills, then busyness is a completely desirable mental and physical state.

96. In each indulgence, congruence should take precedence over quantity. Whatever you choose to engage in, it should be in accordance with your nature and your principles. Your nature should drive you to engage in all of your interests, and your principles should urge you to give complete effort to each. Aim to restrict the quantity of indulgences that do not directly serve your pursuits. Reduce unnecessary indulgences so that you can remain focused on your own ambitions.

Do not extinguish all desire, just employ moderation. Only avoid that which impedes progress or distracts you from pursuing your passions. Desire is necessary to have passion, and you must pursue your passions to find purpose. Therefore, there is great value in desire if you are able to manage your indulgences and filter out those that are incongruent with your nature.

You should forsake arbitrary desires, but do not arbitrarily forsake desires. Do not ignore or suppress desires outright, for you could be snuffing out a beneficial experience. Measure the utility of a given desire before deciding whether to indulge in it. If you find that indulging in something brings you peace of mind, fulfillment, or enrichment, then act on it. If you deem something to be genuinely enriching, then you have identified something that furthers your pursuits. There is no reason to avoid indulging in something enriching just because it is something you desire. Arbitrarily forsaking desires hinders the mind, for if you arbitrarily abandon a course of action, then you will question whether you chose correctly. Alternatively, using reason to elect against a course of action will not bring about feelings of uncertainty or anxious wonder. Avoid clouding your mind with uncertainty and potential regret by reasoning through your desires. Indulge in those that benefit you by furthering your pursuits, and do your best to avoid the rest.

92. No one thing should constantly consume your thoughts. Engage in all of your interests, and be well-rounded so that you avoid resenting your own priorities. Before you know your purpose, you must know your passions, and before that, your interests. Start there. Identify what you are interested in, and work to fulfill every desire that you have to engage with those interests. These sorts of desires are undeniably beneficial and productive in the pursuit of purpose, for you must engage with your interests to develop passions; passions will lead you to purpose. If you arbitrarily choose an interest and forcibly mold it into a passion, then you will stray from the path to

your purpose. Cast a wide net in the search of new experiences by allowing yourself to be busy, multidimensional, and well-rounded. The more exposure you have, the better you can home in on what truly fits your goals and your nature. Not every interest has to become a life-long passion, but you should give each the opportunity to do so.

Engage in each experience, and never deny yourself the opportunity to gain knowledge. If you never forsake these sorts of opportunities, then you will give everything the chance to be interesting. If you are going to spend time doing something, do not waste time convincing yourself that you will not get anything out of it. To say that you cannot learn from an experience is just acknowledging that you lack the skills or focus to do so; your environment can never completely inhibit you from learning and growing.

Any and all experiences have the potential to be learning experiences, so you should strive to learn from every experience you have. That is why you should not arbitrarily filter your interests. The only reason you should not engage with something is if you have already determined that there is a better, more enriching alternative that you should spend your time doing. It is unhealthy to force an interest into becoming a passion or forcing it to define your future, for you will resent your own actions and decisions. By choosing to narrow your realm of engagements, you prevent yourself from fulfilling creative, exploratory desires. Exploration should never be hindered or deterred. If your mind is consumed by only one interest or pursuit, then you will blame any mishaps or mistakes on that one thing. As an athlete, if you were to decide to dedicate all your time and effort to achieving a single goal within your sport, then any setbacks would seem devastating because you would have only one measurement for success, along with a narrow set of goals. Allow your mind to diversify thought and reach in all directions. As a result, you will approach each engagement with a clearer mind and less apprehension.

91. Never expect more of others than you do of yourself. To expect more from others than you do of yourself is to relinquish confidence in your own abilities. There are so many aspects of your character and mindset that are fully within your control. Why should you ever expect anyone to act with more integrity or with more compassion than you? Can you really produce a logical reason to justify an ethical disparity like that? You may justify inaction or wrongdoing by weighing yourself against others, but what use is that? You cannot measure success if your scale for it is constantly changing. You should act without the thought of what you would expect from others. Only then can you start to evaluate successes on a constant, relevant scale. That scale is one determined by your aspirations for the future and by your expectations for your actions in the present.

Additionally, refrain from evaluating others' successes on your scale. Everyone has their own scale for success, and only yours is related to your goals and aspirations. If you were to measure people based on the expectations you have for yourself, then you would always be disappointed and unsatisfied, assuming that you set high expectations for yourself. Falling short of the highest rung is preferable to reaching the top of a shorter ladder. Everyone is climbing their own ladder, and their position on it should not affect how you advance on yours. Here, the height of each ladder is one's expectations for themselves. Some may want an easy, quick path to the top—to meeting expectations—but that is just fabricated success.

Progress is synonymous with success, and satisfaction only comes after experiencing successive successes. To progress, you must move and change in a positive direction, approaching the expectations that you have set for yourself. If you were just sitting at the top of your ladder, you would not be progressing—you would not be succeeding. Yes, reaching the top of the ladder is an indication of past progress and growth, but, in the moment, you would be stagnant. You must continually extend the height of your ladder (raise expectations) so that you always allow yourself the chance to progress. It is satisfying to meet expectations, but how long can your previous successes bring you that satisfaction? When are you going to expect yourself to achieve more? Success is relative to your expectations, and satisfaction is dependent on your perceived level of success. Expectations should be lofty, but attainable. However, lofty expectations should not equate to added pressure. Instead, you should have confidence and surety in raising your expectations because you are doing so only because you have successfully met expectations in the past. Allow your ladder to extend upwards while being confident that you can reach the top rung.

6. Find a purpose for what you do that is bigger than yourself by honoring the sacrifices that others have made for you and taking advantage of every opportunity they provide. You must be ambitious and aware of your desires if you are to eventually arrive at your purpose. If you struggle to find internal motivation to be ambitious, then use gratitude as your fuel. Focus on taking calculated actions to seize the opportunities that others have provided for you, aspiring to honor the sacrifices that they have made to do so.

    Develop your mindset, confidently interact with others in order to form strong relationships, and never deviate from the nature of your character in the pursuit of your ambitions.

EXTRA INNINGS

The final lesson, preceding this epilogue, relays a charge to honor the sacrifices of others, and this book has given me the opportunity to do just that. One way to honor others is to ensure that their legacies endure through you. With the dedication at the beginning of the book and the account to follow, I have the opportunity to remember and honor a former mentor and teacher of mine. I am using this epilogue to articulate his impact and the influence that he had on my life. This book is written in memory of Joel Diffendaffer, who passed away in August 2018. His passing resulted in an added purpose of the book: to aid in the endurance and strength of his legacy.

Joel Diffendaffer (Diff), my high school choir director, was the purest example of someone with a sound mindset, shameless passion, and undying optimism. When I first heard of the news of Diff's passing, I was with my family, and, after a period of silent thought, I told them that something like this should never happen. I said that there is a certain caliber of person that should be guaranteed a full life and that Diff was one of those people. My dad, however, made me realize the ignorance of that statement when he explained that Diff lived life to the fullest each and every day. He did live a full life because of how he lived it. It is always hard to reconcile bad things happening to good people. Well, Diff was the embodiment of good in people, and he was suddenly taken from all of us. The main way that I reconciled this event was by understanding that having more time on this earth does not equate to having a fuller life and that the caliber of a person does not ensure longevity. Instead, the fullness of a life is determined by the caliber of that person.

Tomorrow is never guaranteed, but do not live in fear of it not coming. Instead, approach every new day by assuming a duty to take full advantage of that gift. Nothing was taken from Diff; he was taken from us. The strength of his convictions, coupled with his genuine love and tolerance for others, allowed him to impart an incredibly positive impact on everyone that had the pleasure to meet him. There was no void in Diff's life because he found his purpose and he made a decision to wholeheartedly pursue it. He did so while dutifully interacting with everyone along the way. After every piece in each of our choir concerts, Diff would step off to the side of the stage and point at us, giving us credit and praise. Even though he was the orchestrater—the heart of the entire production—he made us feel that we shared an equal part in creating our sound. He was balanced; humble but driven, calm but focused.

In choir rehearsal, Diff would always say, "we stop to start again." He said it so much that we could predict when he was going to deliver the line. It served as a reminder that there was a purpose to repeating a section of a piece. Restarting was not just so that we could sing the same way over and over; it was so that we could incrementally improve each time. The same mantra has innumerable applications in life: you must stop to reflect, analyze, introspect, and then start again with a new beginning and a refined pursuit.

When I originally wrote the above reflection on Diff, it was August 5, 2018. He had lost his five-day battle the day before, following an aortic dissection. We can all learn from Joel Diffendaffer's approach to life, love, and the pursuit of purpose. He was a special person who inspired many and who was loved by all.

ACKNOWLEDGEMENTS

I have been truly inspired by the unbelievable support and encouragement that I have received throughout the duration of this project. It has compelled me to be more willing to grant my attention, time, and consideration to others' pursuits. Given that this is a self-published title, I relied heavily on the generosity and interest of others in order to get feedback and guidance, and I am beyond grateful for how their contributions helped me progress. I have had numerous people volunteer to jump in, each turning a different gear of this machine. It has all come together so well. Without the help of those mentioned in this section, the book would not be what it is, nor would it have been completed as expediently as it was.

The Pursuit of Purpose is dedicated to my parents and my sister because I attribute the nature of my thought process to my family's teaching and influence—an influence that is overwhelmingly positive. They have been a source of genuine, unrelenting support from the conception of this work to its completion, and I cannot thank them enough.

There are many other friends, family, and acquaintances, whose aid, encouragement, and support I have yet to mention. First, I must give credit for two notable visual contributions to the book. Taylor Whitlock gave life to my sketches of the chapter symbols by putting them in a digital form, employing her borderline obsession with symmetrical precision to nail the design. A professional graphic designer, Gregory Concha, graciously took me on as a client and created the book's cover. He was very responsive and accommodating during that tag-team creative process. In my eyes, these visuals are invaluable, as they greatly enhance the overall presentation and cohesion of this book.

In addition to using the mantra "respect the game," my little league baseball coach, Dan Laskero, imparted another lesson that is fit to frame the following acknowledgements: feedback is a gift. That rule is especially true regarding the writing process; feedback is essential, and I was lucky to have received so much of it.

For preliminary guidance on the format and delivery of my ideas, I would like to thank Donald Leaper and Arik Zeevy—two coaches who have helped strengthen my mind as well as my body.

Giovanna Aguilar has been a utility player when it comes to feedback and guidance. She helped me establish a self-publishing timeline, suggesting that I form a focus group, and advised my promotional efforts. In accordance with her suggestion, I ran a focus group that consisted of close friends of varied backgrounds, ages, and relations. That group proved to be exactly the audience that I needed. For their willing participation in the focus group and for their thoughtful remarks on the book, I thank Bill Zollars, Alex Murtagh, Donald Leaper, Jonathan Felton, Lizzie Spaeth, and Taylor Whitlock.

There is another group of that provided less structured but equally as helpful feedback. They were all very forthcoming with their time and ideas. First, I thank Robert Turtledove for his feedback regarding the concepts presented in the list lessons. By reading, discussing, and challenging a handful of my ideas, Milena Sudarikov helped me refine and bolster my explanations. Finally, for exciting my spirit as an author with his praise of the book, for combing the text for final edits, and for providing the endorsement that is featured on the back cover, I thank Professor Benjamin Ogden.

I am the beneficiary of the overwhelming generosity and compassion of those mentioned above, and I extend my sincerest appreciation to each one for their contributions to what has been the most enriching experience of my life thus far.

ABOUT THE AUTHOR

The Pursuit of Purpose is Garrett Kincaid's debut literary work. He is currently a sophomore in college, studying Quantitative Finance and playing varsity tennis at Stevens Institute of Technology in Hoboken, NJ. Garrett was born and raised in Leawood, KS and attended the Pembroke Hill School in Kansas City, MO. He cites the transition from high school to college as one of the experiences that prompted him to record his thoughts in this book. In addition to writing, his studies, and tennis, Garrett loves to travel, sing, and snow ski.

If you would like to see more from Garrett Kincaid, visit his blog at his website (garrettkincaidauthor.com), and find him on Facebook and Instagram as Garrett Kincaid Author.

Made in the
USA
Middletown, DE

75472746R00090